# À bout de souffle

**CINÉ-FILES: The French Film Guides**
Series Editor: Ginette Vincendeau

From the pioneering days of the Lumière brothers' Cinématographe in 1895, France has been home to perhaps the most consistently vibrant film culture in the world, producing world-class directors and stars, and a stream of remarkable movies, from popular genre films to cult avant-garde works. Many of these have found a devoted audience outside France, and the arrival of DVD is now enabling a whole new generation to have access to contemporary titles as well as the great classics of the past.

The Ciné-Files French Film Guides build on this welcome new access, offering authoritative and entertaining guides to some of the most significant titles, from the silent era to the early twenty-first century. Written by experts in French cinema, the books combine extensive research with the author's distinctive, sometimes provocative perspective on each film. The series will thus build up an essential collection on great French classics, enabling students, teachers and lovers of French cinema both to learn more about their favourite films and make new discoveries in one of the world's richest bodies of cinematic work.

Published and forthcoming Ciné-Files include:

French Film Guide

# À bout de souffle

Ramona Fotiade

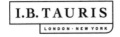

I.B. TAURIS

LONDON · NEW YORK

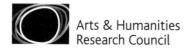

Arts & Humanities
Research Council

This publication is supported by the AHRC.
Each year the AHRC provides funding from the
Government to support research and postgraduate
study in the arts and humanities. Only applications
of the highest quality are funded and the range of
research supported by this investment of public funds
not only provides social and cultural benefits but
also contributes to the economic success of the UK.
For further information on the AHRC, please go to:
www.ahrc.ac.uk

Published in 2013 by I.B.Tauris & Co Ltd
6 Salem Road, London W2 4BU
175 Fifth Avenue, New York NY 10010
www.ibtauris.com

Distributed in the United States and Canada Exclusively by Palgrave Macmillan
175 Fifth Avenue, New York NY 10010

ISBN: 978 1 78076 509 9 (PB)
      978 1 78076 508 2 (HB)

A full CIP record for this book is available from the British Library
A full CIP record is available from the Library of Congress

Library of Congress Catalog Card Number: available

Typesetting and eBook by Tetragon, London
Printed and bound in Great Britain by T.J. International, Padstow, Cornwall

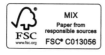

# Contents

# Acknowledgements

The author wishes to thank the AHRC for their assistance in providing an extended period of study leave. Thanks are also due to Ginette Vincendeau for the opportunity of writing a book about a film that I have taught for many years at the University of Glasgow, and that has been a constant source of inspiration for my writing on cinema and postmodernism. I am grateful for the editorial guidance and support that Ginette Vincendeau and Philippa Brewster have provided. My thanks also go to David Scotson in the Learning Technology Unit at the University of Glasgow for his invaluable technical skills. The School of Modern Languages and Cultures at the University of Glasgow funded research trips to Paris. The staff of the Bibliothèque du film (BiFi) and the Institut national de l'audiovisuel (Ina) at the Bibliothèque nationale de France (BnF) in Paris were very helpful in assisting me with locating and accessing printed secondary sources and audio-visual documents.

# Synopsis

The film opens with a sequence set in the old harbour of Marseille. Sun-glassed Michel Poiccard (Jean-Paul Belmondo) hot-wires an American car and drives off to Paris. On his way, he chatters loudly about his plans to collect a sum of money and flee to Italy with his girlfriend. He listens to the radio and plays around with a gun he finds in the glove compartment. Failing to stop at a police check, he is chased by two motorcycle cops, swerves into a country road in an attempt to dodge them, but is caught up when trying to re-start the engine. He picks up the gun from the glove compartment, fires and kills the cop. Early next morning, Michel hitch-hikes to Paris, arriving penniless. He steals money from a former girlfriend (Liliane), who works as a television script girl. He then unsuccessfully tries to find his friend, Tolmatchoff, at the *Agence Interamericana*. Later he meets Patricia Franchini (Jean Seberg), a young American student and aspiring journalist, who sells the *New York Herald Tribune* on the Champs-Élysées. Michel asks her whether she will accompany him to Rome, and they decide to meet again that evening. Back at the *Agence Interamericana*, Tolmatchoff gives Michel a cheque but, because of his recent troubles, Michel can only cash it with the help of another friend, Antonio Berruti. Shortly afterwards, two policemen arrive to question Tolmatchoff. They rush off in pursuit of Michel. In order to pay for his dinner with Patricia that evening, Michel goes into the toilets of a bar where he attacks a man and steals his wallet. Patricia leaves Michel to go to a meeting with an American journalist, and discuss the details of an interview at Orly airport. The next morning, Patricia returns to her hotel room, only to find that Michel has been waiting for her. A long conversation follows, during which Patricia reveals that she may be pregnant. Michel tries several times to phone his friend, Antonio. Eventually, he and Patricia make love and then prepare to go to Patricia's interview at Orly. While Patricia is choosing a new dress for the press conference, Michel steals another car. They are about to drive off when a man in dark glasses (Jean-Luc Godard) recognises Michel's photo in the newspaper and reports this to the police. Patricia takes part in the press conference of the novelist Parvulesco (Jean-Pierre Melville) at Orly. Michel unsuccessfully tries to sell the stolen car to a garage in the suburbs and ends up getting into a fight. At the newspaper offices, Detective Vital questions Patricia and shows her Michel's photograph on the front page of *France-Soir*. She is followed as she leaves, but dodges her pursuer by going into a cinema and leaving through the toilet window. Patricia and Michel go to see a western, then steal a Cadillac in a car park. Later that evening, Michel finds Berruti, who promises to get him the money, and suggests that Michel and Patricia go to spend the night in the flat of a photographer friend. The next morning, Michel asks Patricia to buy a newspaper and get a bottle of milk. She leaves, browses through the newspaper, then goes into a café and calls Detective Vital. Back in the flat, she tells Michel she has just called the police. When Berruti arrives in a convertible with the money, Michel refuses to run away with him. The police car arrives, and Michel is shot in the back and dies.

# Introduction

One of the most charismatic feature films of the New Wave, *À bout de souffle* has retained much of its appeal for contemporary audiences not only as the emphatic statement of a generational break with tradition, but also as Godard's earliest rendition of a set of thematic and stylistic motifs that were going to become his trademark. Released in March 1960, less than a year after Truffaut's *Les Quatre cents coups* [The 400 Blows] and Resnais's *Hiroshima mon amour*, *À bout de souffle* (loosely based on a scenario suggested by Truffaut) was very much a film of its time. Yet, the idiosyncratic treatment of cinematography, montage, dialogue and soundtrack set it apart, heralding the birth of a postmodern *auteur*. Having won the prestigious Jean Vigo award even before its general release, *À bout de souffle* benefited from an unprecedented multimedia publicity campaign, and enjoyed very positive reviews (with only a few exceptions in the specialised press). The sustained critical attention that has made this a cult film over almost 50 years has been propelled by, among other things, the memorable coupling of its leading actors, Jean-Paul Belmondo and Jean Seberg, whose story on screen seemed to portray the troubled love affair between French cinema and Hollywood.

This guide provides a thorough examination of the production and reception contexts of the film, in order to re-assess notions of authorship versus generational affiliation within the New Wave. Most importantly, it situates *À bout de souffle* in relation to Godard's filmography from the 1960s onwards, focusing on the elaboration of a narrative and visual discourse that has come to be identified with a distinctive strand in postmodern French cinema. The recognisable impact of Godard's early counter-narrative and visual strategies on the US independent film production and, later, on the so-called *Cinéma du Look* of the 1980s and 1990s will be considered as part of an ongoing debate about cultural identity and authorial responses to the French versus the American semiotics of film.

Contrary to what some of its critics alleged, *À bout de souffle* was not the work of an amateur director who ignored the rules of continuity editing and the language of classical cinema. Godard's debut feature was acknowledged as the manifesto of the New Wave precisely insofar as it deliberately challenged the tradition of both classical Hollywood cinema and the French filmmaking industry of the time, by establishing a set of revolutionary techniques that became identified with the *politique des auteurs* elaborated during the 1950s in the pages of the *Cahiers du cinéma*. A film about filmmaking and the history of cinema, *À bout de souffle* stages and performs a calculated displacement of editing and storytelling conventions that established Godard as the *Nouvelle Vague auteur par excellence*, and later confirmed his reputation as one of the first postmodern directors in French cinema. This parodic re-appropriation of a classical thriller (dedicated to Monogram Pictures, the American B-movie production company) turned budgetary constraints to its advantage by using outdoor locations, natural lighting, a hand-held camera and a crew reduced to a minimum to create the impression of a more authentic, if stylised, approach to reality. The 'documentary' feel of the cinematography and editing (inspired by ethnographer Jean Rouch's landmark films of the 1940s and 1950s) was counter-balanced by a deliberate play with genre conventions as well as by constant references to both the silent and the classical cinematic codes. The notion and visual 'imprint' of authorial style was thus highlighted as a strategy of imposing the French cultural stance against the dominant Hollywood studio system. Undoubtedly, the collapse of the integrated studio systems on both sides of the Atlantic during the late 1950s and 1960s contributed to the emergence of new methods of production that privileged speed, spontaneity and cost-efficient ideas over the lavish *mise-en-scène* and the inbuilt marketing potential of big budget mainstream movies. Moreover, the availability of lightweight cameras and more light-sensitive film stock bypassed the need for artificial lighting and made shooting on location preferable, which in turn could not fail to have an impact on acting, camera movement, the length of shots and even the number of takes. Notoriously sparing with the latter, Godard tried to achieve the best possible effect in one take, and did not hesitate to ask his cameraman, Raoul Coutard, to use the Ilford HPS stock (normally confined to photographic journalism), as well as the Geva 36 stock for filming in conditions that seemed to defy the technical specifications of the material. 'Even the film stock, you'll see, will be breathless,'[1] Godard wrote to Pierre Braunberger (producer of his short films). In breaking the rules of continuity editing and the logical links or motivations behind different scenes, Godard for the first time drew attention to the film image itself and to the materiality of the medium that gradually gained precedence over the unfolding of a loosely strung-together thriller plot. The idea of re-appropriating a 'conventional story' in order to redefine 'everything that cinema had done'[2] resonates with the self-referentiality and pastiche mood with which postmodernism typically assimilates diachronical or synchronical cultural phenomena. One of the earliest European *auteurs* to use filmic citation in a sustained and programmatic manner, Godard has refined this idiosyncratic practice and elevated it to the status of art, along with his trademark disjunction of the image and the soundtrack. The legendary quotations from Otto Preminger's *Whirlpool* (1949) and Budd Boetticher's *Westbound* (1959) in *À bout de souffle* not only roughly circumscribed the period between his debut as a journalist and his first feature film, but also provided ample opportunity for New Wave private jokes and a more general confrontation between Hollywood classics and French literary heritage (such as modernist poets Guillaume Apollinaire and Louis Aragon, whose verses are oddly substituted for the dubbed soundtrack of

*Westbound*). Along with the provocative insertion of jump cuts into the codified filmic grammar, the palimpsest of cinematic quotations and meta-narrative cues have played a major part in the enduring success of Godard's debut feature which still captivates today's audiences as both a forceful generational statement and an individual postmodern pronouncement about the language and limitations of cinematic representation.

## Notes

1   Jean-Luc Godard, letter to Pierre Braunberger, in Pierre Braunberger, *Cinémamémoire*, Paris: Centre National de la Cinématographie/Centre Georges Pompidou, 1987, p. 184. (All the translations are mine unless otherwise indicated).

2   Jean Narboni and Tom Milne (eds), *Godard on Godard*, translated by Tom Milne, New York and London: Da Capo Press, 1972, p. 173.

# 1 Production Contexts

## Before À bout de souffle

One of the best-known and most controversial directors of the French New Wave, Jean-Luc Godard started off, like many of his generation, as a *cinéphile*, an enthusiastic film buff with a mission. Among the handful of youngsters who regularly attended the screenings at the *Cinémathèque française* during the late 1940s, Godard soon acquired the reputation of a maverick film critic. Following his formative years in the company of such emblematic figures as Rohmer, Rivette and Truffaut, Godard's opinions often ran counter to the freshly established 'orthodoxy' of the *Cahiers du cinéma* team, which paved the way to the official launch of the *Nouvelle Vague* less than a decade later. The intellectual authority of its mentor, and founder of *Cahiers*, André Bazin, did not prevent Godard from expressing a highly individual stand on both technical and ideological issues, despite his acknowledgement of shared interests and mutual respect among the members of the group. 'I have always had, through my education, the spirit of contradiction' – he remarked in an interview with Alain Bergala in 1985. 'I said to myself: they are sharp-tongued, but couldn't one say the opposite? Bazin was saying: sequence-shot, and I was asking myself whether continuity editing was not good, after all. [...] When everyone was berating a film or a director, I used to say to myself: I shall say all the good things that I think of it.'[1] But the opposite was equally true, and Godard's professed independence of opinion came out particularly well in his negative critique of Astruc's *Les Mauvaises Rencontres* [*Bad Liaisons*, 1954], in an unpublished letter to *Cahiers du cinéma*. The author of the landmark essay, 'The Birth of a New Avant-Garde: La Caméra-stylo' (1948), Alexandre Astruc, had become a highly respected critic and filmmaker of the *Cahiers* whom the 24-year-old Godard was taking to task over his choice and treatment of a conventional story. However, Godard's apt remarks on the discrepancy between the ideology and practice of the *caméra-stylo* in Astruc's work went on to be endorsed by film historians and critics such as Roger Boussinot who, in the Bordas *Encyclopedia of the Cinema* (1967), wondered what could be the meaning of the *caméra-stylo* 'when a young *cinéaste* takes his stories from nineteenth-century Normand writers (Barbey, Flaubert, Maupassant)'.[2] This move away from literary adaptations and classical subject matter came to represent a readily identifiable feature of the *Nouvelle Vague*, with ground-breaking first features inspired by autobiographical events (*Les Quatre cents coups*) or sensational news items, *faits divers*, such as Godard's *À bout de souffle*, in the honoured tradition of B-movies and pulp fiction. But even before he acquired his reputation as the *enfant terrible* of the *Nouvelle Vague*, Jean-Luc Godard can be said to have had more than one go at the maverick lifestyle of the young truant and occasional thief that Truffaut himself portrayed, less than a decade on, in his directorial debut.

Born on 3 December 1930, in Paris, the second of four children, Godard came from a wealthy French-Swiss bourgeois milieu against whose values and conceptions he found himself, quite early on, determined to rebel, even if one can say that his early education and voracious appetite for reading benefited from the vast family library and the wide range of cultural interests (from photography to drawing, from music to the cinema, painting and architecture). His father, Paul-Jean, the son of a jeweller, became a prestigious doctor, having studied medicine in France and England. His mother, Odile Monod, was descended from a family of bankers and investors who shared the Protestant faith and the double, French-Swiss, background of Godard's father. Jean-Luc himself was to spend his childhood and most of his adult life between Switzerland and France. As he recalled in an interview with Alain Bergala, in 1985: 'In fact, I have always lived between Switzerland and France. I've always had two countries ever since I was a little boy. I was born in Paris, I came to live here [Switzerland] when I was one year old. At three, I went back to Paris. Then I came back here, where I went to school until the age of thirteen. After that, I went to the Lycée Buffon until the age of twenty. I have always been between the two ...' Godard's sheltered childhood and adolescence as part of an affluent and highly cultivated milieu (his maternal grandfather, Julien-Pierre Monod, was close to André Gide, and a lifelong friend and secretary of Paul Valéry), seemed – at first sight – to set him apart from the majority of the *Nouvelle Vague* aspiring filmmakers: 'I have a feeling that I'm not asking for power or riches or anything, because I had more than plenty until I was fifteen. More than anyone. It was very different from Truffaut, for example', as Godard declared to Colin MacCabe.[3] However, it was not long before the young Godard turned against his strict Protestant upbringing to embark on a life of truancy and petty theft in post-war Paris, where he arrived in 1946 as a student at the Lycée Buffon and a boarder at a pension in the rue d'Assas. Welcomed by the extended Monod family into the high-bourgeois world of Sunday meals and family reunions, Jean-Luc started to steal, and invariably got caught, only to start again, until he eventually landed in prison in Zurich, in 1952, during an episode to some extent reminiscent of the typewriter theft in Truffaut's *Les Quatre cents coups*. His adolescent criminality was mostly a case of petty theft that one would associate with Michel Poiccard's cavalier manners when he visits his friend, Liliane, in *À bout de souffle*. Unusually though, Godard also claims he financed Jacques Rivette's first film, *Le Quadrille* (1950) – in which Godard himself made an appearance – by stealing from an uncle.

To put such affirmations into context, it must be said that this is the time (during the late 1940s and early 1950s) when the future filmmaker undertook an intensive education in cinema by regularly attending the screenings of the *Ciné-Club du Quartier Latin*, where he met Éric Rohmer, Jacques Rivette and François Truffaut. He was equally among the devotees of the *Cinémathèque française*, which acquired its new premises in the avenue de Messine in 1948, and began screening old-time French classics, such as Feuillade's popular serials, along with B-grade American thrillers and westerns produced by the Monogram Pictures company that survived its early demise in the 1950s to enter cinema legend with Godard's famous dedication in the opening credits of *À bout de souffle*.

As significant as the after-screening discussions at the *Cinémathèque*, where Truffaut, Rivette, Godard, Rohmer and Chabrol regularly met, was Godard's decision to register at the Sorbonne, in 1949, for a certificate in anthropology. His first-hand contact with the theories of Claude Lévy-Strauss, and the revolutionary films of Jean Rouch, had an undeniable, if not fully documented, impact on Godard's conception of cinema that film historians and critics have often pondered over. Luc Moullet's perceptive review of *À bout de souffle* (published in *Cahiers du cinéma*, in April 1960) highlighted for the first time the close relationship between Godard's debut feature and Rouch's *Moi, un noir*, *Les Maîtres fous* and *Jaguar*. Godard's passionate interest in Rouch, coupled with Henri Langlois's own appreciation of Surrealism (and of the Surrealists' favourite early productions, such as Feuillade's *Les Vampires*), have led to much speculation on the possible cross-fertilisation between anthropology and the avant-garde's appropriation of primitive culture, as a decisive factor in shaping the ideology of the *Nouvelle Vague*. MacCabe places Structuralism (as the heir of Surrealism and anthropology) and the New Wave among the concurrent manifestations of 'Parisian intellectual and cultural dominance of the West', while wondering about the apparent lack of interaction between 'these two worlds', despite their 'geographical proximity'.[4] Monaco states that, in the years following Godard's registration at the Sorbonne, 'the five *Cahiers* critics were deeply involved in developing what we might call a "structural anthropology" of film [...] expressed in terms of *auteurs* and genres'.[5] Any coherent answer to questions relating to the cultural and ideological context that influenced the making of *À bout de souffle*, would also need to refer to Godard's career as a film critic, and his contributions to *Cahiers du cinéma* in particular.

## Godard the Film Critic

Filmmaking came as a natural extension to writing, in Godard's case. More generally, though, the intimate relationship between writing and directing, literary and cinematic authorship was part of the *politique des auteurs*, promoted by *Cahiers du cinéma* team. It had also been most eloquently brought to light by Astruc's notion of the *caméra-stylo*, in his landmark essay of 1948.[6] As a young man, Godard himself had aspired to become a novelist, and if he gradually turned his attention to cinema, he never lost sight of the significant transition from film criticism to filmmaking that – for him – seemed to relate one type of thinking to another: 'Writing was already making films. […] As a critic, I already considered myself a *cinéaste*' – Godard stated in an interview which came out in 1962, in the special issue of the *Cahiers* devoted to the *Nouvelle Vague*.[7] The range of subjects and *auteurs* that Godard dealt with in his articles of the 1950s (from Russian propaganda films to Hollywood westerns, from Mankiewicz to Bergman, Rossellini to Renoir, not forgetting Hitchcock, Rouch and Mizoguchi) allows one to measure the astounding breadth and depths of his interests at the time. The ideology, the style and the technical innovations for which *À bout de souffle* was hailed as an emblematic *Nouvelle Vague* manifesto upon its release can all be traced back to Godard's carefully positioned, yet passionate, reactions to some of the most influential as well as some of the most obscure, and rightfully forgotten, productions in worldwide cinema. Both art-house and popular films as well as box-office winners and losers attracted his attention, but his choices were nevertheless indicative of a number of *parti pris*, or rather of the self-assured manner in which a set of early preferences and oppositions were to develop and crystallise over the years into a fully fledged conception and practice of the cinema.

The first article that Godard published (in the *Gazette du cinéma* No. 2/1950) was an appreciative review of Joseph Mankiewicz's *House of Strangers* that placed the filmmaker's achievement on a par with novelist Alberto Moravia's literary art, and ended with another literary reference, to the leader of the Surrealist movement, André Breton, who once defined his approach to writing as a way of arranging meetings. Such references, and the occasional mention of the missed or successful *rendez-vous* between authors and their audiences, are scattered throughout Godard's film criticism of the period. An interesting leitmotif of his later films and writings (*Passion, King Lear, JLG/JLG*) related the notion of montage to the Surrealist understanding of the poetic image, inspired by Pierre Reverdy's famous statement that 'an image is the creation of the mind by drawing together two different realities; the further apart the realities, the stronger the image.'[8] However, the formative influence of Surrealism, just as the recurrent comments on the Russian cinema of the 1940s (in particular, on Eisenstein's films), points to the crucial significance that Godard attached, very early on, to montage and *mise-en-scène*. Three articles spell out Godard's idea that great directing resides in an understanding of the different roles and the interaction between montage and *mise-en-scène*. The first, published in the *Gazette du cinéma* (3/1950), bears the rather misleading title 'Towards a Political Cinema', since Godard does not take any definite political stand, but discusses (in typical provocative fashion) both Soviet and Nazi propaganda films in terms of acting, camera movement and memorable images or sequence shots. The second article, entitled 'Defence and Illustration of Classical Construction' [*Défense et illustration du découpage classique*], which came out in *Cahiers du cinéma* on 15 September 1952, was an attack on André Bazin's anti-montage theory that can be attributed to Godard's fiercely independent views during his formative period, although it also clearly anticipated his lifelong commitment to innovative montage as a means of heightening reality rather than an end in itself. The more flexible, if idiosyncratic, interpretation of classical *découpage*, or continuity editing, that Godard ultimately proposed in his article, excluded neither Renoir's use of deep focus in *Madame Bovary* and *La Règle du jeu* [The Rules of the Game], nor the occasional 'ten minutes take' – which was set to become a trademark of Godard's filmmaking, after featuring prominently in *À bout de souffle*.

The third and most important article in the series, 'Montage, My Fine Care' [*Montage, mon beau souci*] (published in *Cahiers du cinéma* No. 65, in December 1956), emphasised Godard's idea that 'montage is above all an integral part of *mise-en-scène*', while at the same time distinguishing between the former's preoccupation with time, as opposed to the latter's spatial elaboration. The importance of the eye-line match, in particular, brings out Godard's understanding of good montage practice, and of its close relationship with *mise-en-scène*:

> Cutting on a look is almost the definition of montage, its supreme ambition as well as its submission to *mise-en-scène* [...] The famous sequence of the cymbals in the remake of *The Man Who Knew Too Much* is the best proof. Knowing just how long one can make a scene last is already montage, just as thinking about transitions is part of the problem of shooting.[9]

Further on, Godard remarks that 'a brilliantly directed film gives the impression of having simply been placed end to end, but a film brilliantly edited gives the impression of having suppressed all direction'. The differences between French and English film terminology are not made to simplify things, and it is worth pointing out that *mise-en-scène* in the first case (as in 'un film génialement mis en scène') refers indeed to directing (and implicit authorial input), unlike the final mention of *mise-en-scène* ('l'impression d'avoir supprimé toute *mise-en-scène*'), which more adequately corresponds to the English notion of continuity within the frame, and the importance of what the frame contains, as opposed to editing and montage.

As in his previous 'Defence and Illustration of Classical Construction', in 'Montage, My Fine Care' Godard is first advocating the qualities of continuity editing or classical *découpage*, whose very principle of unseeming transitions appears ingrained in the unity of the frame, before moving on to hail the expressive value of montage:

> In other words, to give the impression of duration through movement, of a close shot through a long shot, is one of the aims of *mise-en-scène* and the opposite of one of those of montage. [...] Cutting a camera movement in four may prove more effective than keeping it as [a] shot. An exchange of glances, to revert to our previous example, can only be expressed with sufficient force – when necessary – by editing.[10]

Again, the difficulties of translation obscure Godard's emphasis on montage in this passage, which, in French, ends with a reference to 'a skilful montage effect' [*un adroit effet de montage*] rather than to 'editing', which is lacking in precision, as it encompasses all processes of assembling the film, from shooting stage to post-production and final cut. Conversely, 'montage' is widely considered to designate the editing together of several brief shots, aiming to achieve a strong emotional impact, and often to show a contraction or expansion of time and/or space.[11] This particular understanding of the term corresponds to Godard's distinctive use of jump cuts and striking transitions between scenes in *À bout de souffle* that highlight his equally personal alternation of very brief shots and long takes, creating a recognisable rhythm. Fully aware of the importance that such 'rhythm' acquires in defining an author's *style*, Godard does not hesitate (when writing for instance his article 'Bergmanorama', published in *Cahiers* in 1958) to divide the directors he admires into those who tend to use the construction of the film and montage to express their views, and those who excel in their use of *mise-en-scène*. In the first category, Godard placed Rossellini and Welles; in the second, Hitchcock and Lang. This may seem rather contradictory given not only Hitchcock's celebrated use of cutting on the gaze but also Godard's own previous admission (in 'Montage, My Fine Care') that 'montage is above all an integral part of *mise-en-scène*'. However, any such statement needs to be placed in the context of Godard's unfailing allegiance to Italian Neo-Realism, and to Rossellini in particular, as distinct from Truffaut's equally strong endorsement of Hitchcock. If the ensuing opposition between Bergman, who 'belongs to the cinema of freedom', and Visconti, who represents a 'cinema of rigour', may appear to complicate matters further, this is only because from Godard's point of view, Bergman like Rossellini are in a class of their own. While praising Bergman's readiness to take risks and 'advance into unknown lands' as contrasted to Visconti's technical prowess and flawless *mise-en-scène*, Godard is clearly anticipating the defining choices he will have to make for his directorial debut: 'Personally I prefer *Summer with Monika* and *Senso*, and the *politique des auteurs* to the *politique des metteurs en scène*'.[12] This concluding remark confirms an evolution in Godard's conception that was gradually taking shape in his three previous articles on *mise-en-scène* and montage. The initial concern with camera movement, lighting, *décor* and acting (all elements of *mise-en-scène* that were prominent in 'Towards a Political Cinema') makes way for a sustained analysis of montage and its ability to enhance the continuity or unity of individual frames, as illustrated in Godard's subsequent articles. It is possible that his spell in the film industry during the mid-1950s, when he worked as an editor on travel films for Arthaud, gave him a better understanding of post-production processes and – most significantly – equipped him with hands-on experience of montage. However, his uncompromising remarks about the style of famous directors such as Rossellini, Hitchcock and Lang show that his personal understanding of the *auteur* and of the *politique des auteurs* was closely associated with the expressive value of montage even in the case of filmmakers he admired mainly for their outstanding *mise-en-scène*. Moreover, when comparing the unprecedented use of jump cuts in *À bout de souffle* to Godard's articles of the 1950s, one can say that his break-away from conventional editing did not result from a dilettante's lack of experience, but rather from the critic's in-depth knowledge of the principles and evolution of continuity editing from the early silent era to the classical Hollywood cinema. The status that his first feature-length film acquired as a manifesto of the *Nouvelle Vague* must therefore be measured up against Godard's explicit defence or, more adequately, against his proven critical awareness of the role and limitations of continuity editing, as well as of *mise-en-scène*, and of the full range of expressive means that articulated the established language of cinema at the time.

Another aspect of the existing French filmmaking practice that Godard wittingly set out to undermine in *À bout de souffle* related to the crippling constraints that the cameraman and the team of technicians often imposed on the director during shooting. In his interview with Éric Rohmer, published in *Les Amis du cinéma* (1/1952), Godard carefully edges his interlocutor's reflections towards a decisive final comment, in which no one can fail to recognise a New Wave directorial 'statement of intentions':

GODARD: You have, I believe, a technical supervisor assigned to you?

ROHMER: Yes. My chief complaint about him, and about my lighting cameraman, is that they slow down the shooting by worrying too much about certain taboos. The real lesson of Italian cinema has not yet been generally understood. It really is incredible when a cameraman says to you: 'Don't do that, I couldn't light it. Don't have your actors move too much or I'll have to redo my lighting.' The plain fact is that our cameramen lack courage and they aren't going to get it from schools like E.T.P.C. or I.D.H.E.C. Quite the contrary.[13]

Godard's successful collaboration for *À bout de souffle* with his cameraman, Raoul Coutard, was based on their common acknowledgment that the principles of the old French school of cinema (taught in establishments such as the École technique de photographie et de cinématographie [ETPC] and the Institut des hautes études cinématographiques [IDHEC]) had become anachronistic, and needed to be replaced by a fresh and more spontaneous approach to filmmaking.

Raoul Coutard's own recollection of the shooting of *À bout de souffle* (in an article published in the *Nouvel Observateur* in 1965)[14] echoed Godard's views, and confirmed their shared belief in the timely advent of New Wave techniques which added a revolutionary practice to the iconoclastic theory of the *politique des auteurs*.

No survey of Godard's activity as a film critic would be complete without a mention of the constant interplay of cinematic and literary quotations, which gradually and almost imperceptibly spilled over into the composition of his short and feature-length films to become part of his directorial style. Over the past five decades, the postmodern appropriation and displacement of visual and textual fragments has established a subtle relationship between his film criticism and filmmaking, as if one form of commentary takes over where the other one leaves off. Quoted twice in his articles of the 1950s, a quatrain by Surrealist Louis Aragon comes up unexpectedly in *À bout de souffle*, when an off-screen voice recites it during a supposedly dubbed version of a Western that Jean Seberg and Belmondo watch, as they take refuge from the police in a cinema: 'In the crossway of kisses / The years pass too quickly / Beware beware beware / Shattered memories'. The first time Godard quoted the poem was in a short and disapproving note on *La Ronde* by Max Ophuls (published in *Gazette du cinéma*, 4/1950). The second time, Aragon's quatrain concluded an enthusiastic review of Jacques Rozier's *Blue Jeans* as part of a lengthy discussion of the best French productions in the Short Film Festival of Tours in 1959 (published in *Cahiers du cinéma* only six months before the shooting of *À bout de souffle* began). Significantly, Godard's avowed preference and admiration for documentaries (such as Alain Resnais's *Le Chant du Styrène*) or short fiction films on contemporary topics (such as Rozier's *Blue Jeans*) stand out against his cursory dismissal of bland literary adaptations, such as *La Ronde*. In retrospect, *À bout de souffle* illustrates not only Godard's fidelity to a range of literary and cinematic sources (among which Cocteau, Aragon and – more generally – Surrealism are often cited), but also his interest in the spontaneity of filming techniques that the French documentary cinema pioneered (most notably in Jean Rouch's ethnographic productions). Several articles which Godard published between January and July 1959, shortly before he embarked on the making of *À bout de souffle*, explicitly placed the New Wave recent films (from Truffaut's *Les Quatre cents coups* to Chabrol's *Les Cousins* [The Cousins] or Resnais and Marker's *Les Statues meurent aussi* [Statues Also Die]) in the same lineage as Rossellini's Neo-Realism and Jean Rouch's documentaries, to the point of declaring in a review of *Moi, un noir*: 'All great fiction films tend towards documentary, just as all great documentaries tend towards fiction.'[15]

Ultimately, it is not surprising that a couple of years after the success of *À bout de souffle*, during the shooting of *Les Carabiniers* (his third feature film), Godard re-asserted the close aesthetic and ideological relationship between film-writing and filmmaking:

Today I still think of myself as a critic, and in a sense I am, more than ever before. Instead of writing criticism, I make a film, but the critical dimension is subsumed. I think of myself as an essayist, producing essays in novel form, or novels in essay form: only instead of writing, I film them. Were cinema to disappear, I would simply accept the inevitable and turn to television; were television to disappear, I would revert to pencil and paper. For there is a clear continuity between all forms of expression. It's all one.[16]

### First Short Films: From Acting and Editing to Directing

During the mid- to late 1950s, Godard moved from writing to filmmaking, and authored several short films, the first of which was – significantly – a documentary. Given the considerable influence that the French ethnographic and documentary film school had on the *Nouvelle Vague*, it is worth mentioning that the young critics at *Cahiers du cinéma* came into contact with Jean Rouch's work as early as 1949 when Godard, Rivette and Truffaut, alongside many others, attended the *Festival du film maudit* [the Festival of the Cursed Film] at Biarritz, presided over by Cocteau. Rouch's film, *Initiation à la danse des possédés* [Initiation into Possession Dance], shot in Niger, was awarded the first prize, and another of his shorts, *Circumcision*, filmed in Mali, won the Prix du Reportage at the Misguich Festival the same year. Although Godard's enthusiastic articles on *Moi, un noir* (published in *Arts* and *Cahiers du cinéma*) date back to 1959, Rouch's films had most certainly been known to him for about a decade. One must not forget that it was in the autumn of 1949 that Godard registered to study anthropology at the Sorbonne, a decision possibly prompted by his recent experience of the Biarritz festival, and most certainly endorsed by Théodore Monod, a family relation and leading French anthropologist who incidentally played a major part in Rouch's early career. Some of the most distinctive aesthetic and technical innovations credited to the *Nouvelle Vague* were originally developed by the documentary filmmakers in response to the often improvised or precarious conditions of shooting they found themselves confronted with; thus, Rouch's hand-held camera, the post-synchronised commentary and the compelling montage of *Moi, un noir* (all aspects commented on at length by Godard) provided practical answers to the use of a Rolleiflex camera without a tripod, to the absence of light portable sound recording equipment, or to the extremely short – 20 seconds – reel of film that forced the director to edit his film while shooting, as Rouch pointed out.[17]

In 1951, after a year spent travelling around South America with his father or on his own, Godard returned to France and was later persuaded by his parents to take up a job working for a company that constructed dams in the Swiss Alps. Following another appointment, with Swiss television, in 1952, and an embarrassing brush with the law on account of stealing from his employers, which led to Godard's short spell in prison and his internment (at his father's advice) in a mental asylum outside Lausanne, the only solution for the young man who had by then severed almost all family ties was to go back to the Grande Dixence, the building site in the Swiss Alps. This time, he used the opportunity to save enough of his wages in order to be able to make a short documentary film on the construction of the dam. *Opération béton* [Operation Concrete], which was completed in the summer of 1954 with the help of a camera operator whom Godard met in Lausanne, Adrien Porchet, lasted seventeen minutes and had the advantage of being shot in 35mm (as compared to the amateur 16mm format adopted by other first-time directors at *Cahiers*). Having post-synchronised the film, and added a classical music score (by Bach and Handel), Godard managed to sell it to the construction company, and thus find the means not only to subsist for the next couple of years but also to finance another film project. *Opération béton* was certainly not in the same league as groundbreaking documentaries such as Buñuel's *Las Hurdes* (1937), and had nothing that foreshadowed Godard's later evolution, apart from the manner in which it seems to resonate with the author's avowed veneration for Rouch and his strong allegiance to the *Nouvelle Vague* documentary and short film French team present at the Tours festival in 1959.

For his second project, Godard borrowed a camera from the distributors of *Opération béton*, Actua Films,[18] and decided to adapt a nineteenth-century story, 'Le Signe', by Guy de Maupassant. The choice is surprising to a certain extent – in view of Godard's critical remarks at the time concerning Astruc's and even Rohmer's interest in classical literary texts. However, the resulting 16mm short, *Une femme coquette*, made in November 1955, represented Godard's first attempt at shooting a fiction film, as well as the occasion to explore a number of themes that were to become part of his personal repertoire over the years – in particular, women's condition and prostitution. The main character in the story, a married woman, uses a prostitute's body language, 'the sign', in order to pick up a man. Only ten minutes long, *Une femme coquette* featured Marie Lysandre, Roland Tolmatchoff and Godard himself as cast members. Godard had previously acted in Rohmer's short, *Charlotte et son steak* (a.k.a. *Présentation*), one of several instalments in the 'Charlotte and Véronique' series,[19] in which both young directors eventually got involved and continued to work, either in collaboration or independently during the mid- to late 1950s. For his part, Godard made *Charlotte et Véronique* (subtitled *All Boys Are Called Patrick*) in 1957, on a scenario by Rohmer, and *Charlotte et son Jules*, which he single-handedly scripted, directed and dubbed, in 1958.

Despite the obvious similarities displayed by the films in the series, there is something that sets Godard's two shorts apart from the rest: they were actually professionally produced by Pierre Braunberger, a celebrated figure in French cinema, who had extensive experience (working with Renoir, Gide and Marc Allégret among others), and whom Cocteau had asked to help organise the *Festival du film maudit* in Biarritz. As Braunberger recalled:

My meeting with Godard took place in 1955 when Marc Allégret introduced us. His parents were Protestant and owners of a huge clinic in Switzerland. They were friends of Marc's father, the pastor Allégret. They had sent Jean-Luc to Paris where he stayed with Marc.[20]

Incidentally, the 'Protestant clan' of Paris (including Gide, Allégret, but also Jean Schlumberger, in whose house Godard lodged in 1949) seems to have played an important part in the young *cinéaste*'s career. As Colin MacCabe remarked: 'It would not be an exaggeration to say that in the nineteenth century [Godard's maternal family, the Monods] were the single most eminent family of the French Protestant faith'.[21] In any case, it was in Allégret's house that Godard met Anne Colette and Nicole Berger, the two actresses who were to embody Charlotte and Véronique on the screen. A moral tale in the spirit of Rohmer's celebrated work from the 1960s onwards, the scenario for *Charlotte et Véronique* rested on a similar, if slightly more evolved, three-character plot as the one for *Charlotte et son steak*. Two girls who miss each other at a *rendez-vous* in the Luxembourg gardens happen to run into the same young man, the eponymous Patrick (played by Jean-Claude Brialy), and each of them in turn accepts the invitation to see him again in the next couple of days. Back in the flat that they share, the girls excitedly talk about their different encounters, only to discover as they are strolling around Paris together the next day that Patrick is romancing yet another girl with whom he leaves in a taxi, with hardly a backward glance and a hapless shrug for Charlotte and Véronique. Godard's filming brought out the full comic potential of this case of mistaken identity, while anticipating on a number of visual motifs and thematic concerns that made *À bout de souffle* an iconic debut movie over the coming decades. On several occasions, the *mise-en-scène* and the dialogue include striking references to the cinema or to the *cinéphile* group of friends around Rohmer and Godard. A man seated at a café table next to Patrick and Charlotte reads the film magazine *Art*, whose headline reproduces the title of Truffaut's polemical article (published in May 1957): 'French Cinema Is Collapsing Under False Legends'. This scene closely matches the one in *À bout de souffle*, when a girl is trying to sell a copy of *Les Cahiers du cinéma* to Michel Poiccard, shortly after he has passed in front of a cinema where an American action movie, *Ten Seconds to Hell* (released in 1959) is running. The newspaper seller who insistently proposes *France-Soir* to Véronique in *Charlotte et Véronique* similarly reminds one of the ominous role that the French daily plays in the unfolding drama of Poiccard's final forty-eight hours in *À bout de souffle*. More significantly still, the bathroom in Charlotte and Véronique's flat is decorated with a large poster of James Dean in *Rebel Without a Cause* (1955), whose influence on *À bout de souffle* has often been remarked upon, given Godard's avowed veneration for director Nicholas Ray. Apart from implicitly dating and adding authenticity to the events in the film, the constant allusions to the cinema signal what was to become a trademark of Godard's style: his constant cross-references to other films, his self-referential use of the camera and the actors (including numerous cameo appearances from himself). Photographed in black and white by Michel Latouche, *All Boys Are Called Patrick* also featured for the first time the recurring use of striped patterns and the occasional hints at modern painting that marked the *mise-en-scène* of the longest sequence in *À bout de souffle*. The pattern of the wallpaper in Charlotte and Véronique's flat, at the beginning of the film, comes up again in the bathroom scene towards the end, when Véronique – who is wearing a T-shirt with horizontal stripes – hides behind a towel with vertical stripes, as Charlotte is pointing a toy gun at her. Patricia's T-shirt in *À bout de souffle* brings out the same visual play on horizontal and vertical lines when she is seated on the bed in her hotel room, next to Michel wearing a striped bathrobe. In both cases, Godard's compelling repetition of this visual motif seems to echo Buñuel's intriguing use of similar patterns (on the ubiquitous box with striped lines containing a striped tie) in *Un chien andalou*, a film which was also incidentally produced by Pierre Braunberger. Whether a deliberate hint to an admired Surrealist master or an incidental exercise in style the emphasis on striped patterns in the *mise-en-scène* of intimate scenes (set in the bedroom and the bathroom) seems redolent with repressed desire and incommunicability between the sexes. The presence of posters with reproductions of Picasso's drawings, as well as the implicit reference to American thrillers (e.g. Véronique compares Patrick with Cary Grant) further reinforce the similarities in the *mise-en-scène* and the cultural backdrop of *All Boys Are Called Patrick* and *À bout de souffle*.

Michel Latouche worked as a cameraman on Godard's next two shorts, *Charlotte et son Jules* and *Une histoire d'eau*, both produced by Pierre Braunberger and shot in 1958. *Charlotte et son Jules* starred Jean-Paul Belmondo and Anne Colette, in a twenty-minute sketch filmed in Godard's hotel room in rue de Rennes, which strikingly anticipates the better-known sequence with Belmondo and Jean Seberg in *À bout de souffle*. Written by Godard, this final episode in the Charlotte series displays the light tone and simple storyline of the preceding instalments. Charlotte pays a short visit to the flat of her former boyfriend, and finds herself drowned under a barrage of disjointed remarks, in turn reproachful, patronising, sentimental, begging and scornful. Hardly able to utter more than monosyllabic replies, Charlotte smiles, shrugs, and, just as she is about to leave, eventually manages to inform her Jules, with perfect comic timing, that she has only returned to get her toothbrush. Jules's one-way conversation, framed by Charlotte's unexpected arrival (in her new boyfriend's convertible) and her precipitated departure, clearly foreshadows the problems of communication that haunt Patricia and Michel's relationship in *À bout de souffle*. As Michel remarks during his last night with Patricia, in the Swedish photographer's studio: 'Whenever we talked, I talked about myself, and you talked about yourself. [...] But you should have talked about me, and me about you.' The implicit identification between Godard and the male protagonists of his early films is most compellingly brought forward by Belmondo's monologue in *Charlotte et son Jules*, which Godard ended up dubbing with his own voice when the actor was drafted for military service in Algeria. According to Truffaut, 'Jean-Luc's intonations [made] this little film more moving, less relaxed than it would have been had Belmondo dubbed himself,[22] and thus – one could add – harked back to the more wistful mood of Rohmer's *Charlotte et son steak*, in which Godard himself played the lead.

Dubbing and montage similarly bear out Godard's creative imprint on *Une histoire d'eau* [A Story of Water, 1961] which started off as Truffaut's project of a documentary-style fiction inspired by the flooding of the Parisian region in 1958. Pierre Braunberger suggested the documentary approach and provided Truffaut with the film stock, just as he had lent Godard the camera and film stock for *Charlotte et son Jules*. The initial silent footage (which featured Jean-Claude Brialy and Caroline Dim in a haphazard journey across the flooded countryside) yielded spectacular results, but Truffaut – by then busy making his first feature, and editing his short, *Les Mistons* – abandoned the project. Godard took over and turned the disparate rushes into a highly personal film, not only through an ingenious montage (which seems closer than ever before to the unpredictable cuts and transitions in *À bout de souffle*), but also through the stylised use of sound and voice-over narration. Mainly performed by the female lead (Caroline Dim), with occasional interruptions from the male protagonist (dubbed in by Godard), the voice-over discourse provides only a superficial unifying principle, while highlighting the discontinuous and improvised nature of the fictional plot added to the documentary footage. Having hitched a lift with Jean-Claude Brialy, the young woman describes their difficult progress on their way to Paris, but also mixes snippets of dialogue in reported speech with personal stream of consciousness remarks, which interestingly lead up to an explicit homage of the 'art of digression'. The anecdote she recounts about Surrealist Louis Aragon's forty-five-minute eulogy of Matisse during a lecture supposedly devoted to Petrarch occasions a statement that points to the method at work in *Une histoire d'eau*, and which Godard will increasingly make into a *profession de foi* in years to come: 'All of Petrarch's originality lay precisely in his mastery of the art of digression. It's the same for me: I never digress from the point. Or rather, if I seem to, it is because this was my profound subject.'

Incidentally, Jean Rouch successfully used the same post-synchronisation technique in a couple of ethnographic films of the same period which Braunberger produced and Godard enthusiastically reviewed in the *Cahiers*. Rouch's *Jaguar* (1957) and *Moi, un noir* (1958) featured voice-over commentaries improvised by the protagonists to provide a narrative thread to documentary footage. Apart from enhancing the drama documentary feel, the dialogue and narration in *Une histoire d'eau* brim with idiosyncratic literary and cinematic references (e.g. Raymond Chandler, Arthur Gordon Pym, Mack Sennett, Eluard, Giraudoux, Hölderlin etc.) that identify the voice-over discourse as Godard's own. Equally personal is the constant disruption of the image-sound synchronicity that Godard continued to explore from the mid-1960s onwards as part of his visual and narrative strategies. The musical score – in particular the recurring rhythmical drum beat which accompanies the aerial views of the flooding – further suggests possible cross-references with Man Ray's early Surrealist short, *Les Mystères du château du dé* (1929) which Braunberger produced.[23] The spoken credits at the end of *Une histoire d'eau* anticipate the better-known occurrence of the same device in *Le Mépris* (1963). Ultimately, due to the combined effects of montage, soundtrack and fragmented narrative, *Une histoire d'eau* can be said to remain one of Godard's most revealing early experiments.

If historians and critics have been only too swift in dismissing Godard's first shorts for their apparent lack of technical prowess, slim characterisation or poor acting, it is nevertheless significant to consider that, at the time of their first release, they functioned as much-needed illustrations of the manner in which the emerging *Nouvelle Vague* '*auteur*' theory was to be translated into practice. Having been not only the director, but also the scriptwriter, editor and – occasionally – even the producer of most of his early films, Godard acquired an in-depth understanding and experience of all the processes involved in making a film, which would enable him to revolutionise cinematic language and provoke long-lasting changes in the conventions of shooting, acting and montage.

### From Idea to the Shooting Script: Writing *À bout de souffle*

In November and December 1952, the tabloids *France-Soir* and *Détective* published the sensational story of Michel Portail, a young man imprisoned for armed robbery then expelled from the United States, who – after his return to France – spent the summer with his American girlfriend, Beverly Lumet, on the Côte d'Azur, living the high life among cinema stars until the day he decided to steal a Ford Mercury in front of the Greek Embassy so that he could go to Le Havre to see his dying mother. On his way to Brittany, Portail shot a motorcycle policeman and was eventually turned in to the police by his girlfriend. The story caught the attention of Truffaut who, in turn, managed to get producer Pierre Braunberger interested. However, the project did not get off the ground, as Truffaut started instead jotting down ideas for his first feature, *Les Quatre cents coups*. Following a long conversation with Godard at the Richelieu-Drouot metro station in December 1956, Truffaut wrote a sketchy outline of the Portail story, in which the protagonist, having missed the last train from Paris to Le Havre, steals a car near the Saint-Lazare station, and ends up shooting the policeman who is chasing after him on a motorcycle. He then goes to meet his girlfriend, Betty, a young American journalist, and the chase continues in the streets of Paris, from one cinema to the next. Betty is arrested and turns in Michel, who has sought refuge on a barge. When the police arrive, Michel gives himself up but tells them he has swallowed a fatal dose of aspirin. Nobody believes him but once inside the police station, Michel collapses and dies. This synopsis was submitted for approval to the CNC (Conseil national de la cinématographie) on 25 June 1959 and corresponds to the text published in 1997 in *La Lettre du cinéma* No. 3. Another, considerably longer and very detailed treatment, also attributed to Truffaut, was published in *L'Avant-Scène du cinéma* No. 79 in March 1968. Closer to a continuity script with the exception of dialogues, this version matches the locations and most of the narrative developments in the finished film, sometimes down to the smallest details. Although Michel Poiccard is called Lucien, the opening sequence has been moved to Marseille, where the young man 'is pretending to read *Paris Flirt*' while 'watching the traffic in front of the Vieux Port'. The same stunning similarities with Godard's own *découpage* apply to the rest of the script, including fleeting episodes such as the traffic accident which Poiccard witnesses in the streets of Paris, his fascination with Humphrey Bogart's photograph, or his encounter with a student 'selling pamphlets' who asks him whether he has 'something against youth'. The American girlfriend's name is no longer Betty, she is called Patricia, and she sells the *New York Herald Tribune* on the Champs-Élysées. Nevertheless, Godard's contribution was ultimately a lot more substantial than in the case of his previous collaboration with Truffaut on *Une histoire d'eau*. Although willing to follow the outline provided by Truffaut, Godard decided to preserve full authorial control over the dialogues: 'If you have the time to round out in three lines the idea for a film started at the Richelieu-Drouot metro station (those were the good old days), though I don't have access to Françoise Sagan, I can whip up the dialogues'[24] – he wrote to Truffaut. During the 1950s, Godard had written the dialogues for three films that did not get shot (i.e. two scenarios by Edouard Molinaro and director Jean-Pierre Mocky's feature entitled *Mourir à Berlin*). He had also been employed to write the dialogues for Pierre Schoendoerffer's *Pêcheur d'Islande* [a.k.a. *Ramuntcho*] by the future producer of *À bout de souffle*, Georges de Beauregard, whom Godard met when he was press officer at Fox. Given his experience, Godard was confident enough to work on the scenario that Truffaut agreed to send to Beauregard in 1959, with an explicit endorsement of the project, on the strength of the recent success of *Les Quatre cents coups* at the Cannes festival.

Finally Godard's alterations to the original treatment extended further than the development of two scenes barely sketched out by Truffaut (i.e. the twenty-five-minute dialogue between Michel and Patricia in her hotel room and their last night together in the Swedish photographer's studio). The day before the shooting of *À bout de souffle* began, Godard hinted at a number of changes to the continuity script that were likely to surprise Truffaut:

> I'll have you read the continuity in a few days. After all, it's your screenplay. I think you'll be surprised once again. Roughly speaking, the subject will be the story of a boy who thinks of death and of a girl who doesn't. The adventures are those of a car thief (Melville will introduce me to specialists) in love with a girl who sells the *New York Herald* and who takes French civilization courses.[25]

The involvement of Jean-Pierre Melville, himself director of two crime films, most notably *Bob le flambeur* [Bob the Gambler, 1955], points to Godard's admiration for classic American gangster movies, a passion shared by most young *cinéphiles* and contributors to the *Cahiers*. Godard replaced Truffaut's opening citation from Stendhal ('We are going to speak of dreadful things') with a dedication to Monogram Pictures.[26] Most significantly, he changed the ending of Truffaut's scenario, which had Poiccard flee in Berruti's car while hurling insults at Patricia, who does not understand him 'because her French is still not very good'. The initial impulse of making a film in the tradition of American gangster movies once again guided Godard's choice of ending:

> What caused me a lot of trouble was the end. Should the hero die? To start with, I intended to do the opposite of, say, *The Killing*: the gangster would win and leave for Italy with his money. But as an anti-convention it was too conventional […] Finally, I decided that as my avowed ambition was to make an ordinary gangster film, I had no business deliberately contradicting the genre: he must die.[27]

According to Truffaut, Godard's decision was dictated to a greater extent by his dark mood at the time of shooting the film, rather than by the conventions of American *film noir*:

> Jean-Luc chose a violent end because he was by nature sadder than I. He was in the depths of despair when he made that film. He needed to film death, and he had need of that particular ending. I asked him to cut only one phrase which was absolutely horrible. At the end, when the police are shooting at him one of them said to his companion: 'Quick, in the spine!' I told him, 'You can't leave that in.' I was very vehement about it. He deleted the phrase.[28]

Besides a cameo appearance (in celebrated Hitchcock-style) as the passer-by who denounces Poiccard to the police, Godard also added a number of implicit references to his immediate entourage and to his favourite directors and films at the time. The protagonist is christened Michel – originally the name of the Inter-Americana agent in Truffaut's script, whom Godard chose to call Tolmatchoff, in memory of a long-time Swiss friend and impassioned *cinéphile*. The famous novelist that Patricia interviews at Orly bears the name of a young Romanian émigré whom Godard met at the Sorbonne-based Institute of Cinematography in 1949 (Jean Parvulesco). Initially, Jean-Pierre Melville, who played the part, was supposed to impersonate Rossellini, the much admired Italian Neo-Realist director, whose example the *Cahiers* team aspired to emulate.

Eventually, the script of *À bout de souffle*, with a formal endorsement from Chabrol and Truffaut (acting as 'artistic adviser' and 'scriptwriter' respectively),[29] was accepted by Georges de Beauregard, and the shooting began on 17 August 1959. In only four weeks, Godard finished filming on location, in Marseille, on the 'Nationale 7' highway and in different parts of Paris.

### Production and Casting

Although Godard's first short films had benefited from Pierre Braunberger's experience and investment in new talent, it was a younger producer, Georges de Beauregard, who eventually produced À bout de souffle. Born in Marseille in 1920, Beauregard started off as a journalist and founded a short-lived press agency, Universal Press, after the Second World War. Having specialised in the distribution of French and American films in Spain, he emigrated to Barcelona in 1951, where he became acquainted with Raymond Delabre, the owner of the Inter-Americana company, whose name Godard ingeniously used to designate both Tolmatchoff's travel agency and the implicit affinities between the French New Wave and Hollywood classic thrillers in À bout de souffle. In 1956, Godard took over from Chabrol as press and publicity representative at Fox, one of the major Hollywood film corporations. Two years later, he met Beauregard during the presentation of La Passe du diable at Fox:

> At the end of the screening, only one person stood up, a bearded gentleman, in fact more unshaven than bearded, his eyes hidden behind dark glasses, who said to Beauregard very directly, 'Your film is a load of shit' [Votre film est dégueulasse]. It was Jean-Luc Godard who was working then in the Fox press office. He said it without any nastiness because Jean-Luc was intelligent and nice, but he had a rather brusque way of explaining himself. [Beauregard] who had a nose for both people and things [...] was not annoyed by this interchange. On the contrary that was the birth of a long and enduring friendship.[30]

Despite the failure of La Passe du diable (directed by Schoendoerffer), Beauregard embarked on two literary adaptations for the screen with the same director and entrusted the dialogues for the second project, Pêcheur d'Islande, to Godard. Both films (Ramuntcho [1958] and Pêcheur d'Islande [1959]) were total flops, and left Beauregard on the edge of bankruptcy, with no less than 600,000FF of debt. As Godard's memorable tribute to Georges de Beauregard bears witness, the producer who managed to get the funding for À bout de souffle was himself in dire straits, perpetually fighting 'the ogre at the bank, the dragon at the CNC, more often KO than victorious'.[31] The man who 'produced Belmondo's first smile [À bout de souffle] and Bardot's last [Le Mépris]'[32] (according to Godard), accepted the gamble and succeeded in persuading René Pignières, a major distributor, and Gérard Beytout, a producer with money in the CNC bank, to invest 510,000FF in Godard's first feature. According to Pierre Risient, Godard's assistant for À bout de souffle, the only security awarded for the otherwise modest sum (a fraction of the normal cost of any French film at the time) came from the recent success of Truffaut's Les Quatre cents coups and Resnais's Hiroshima mon amour at the Cannes festival in 1959. Suddenly, every distributor and producer wanted 'his New Wave film', with the names of Truffaut and Chabrol attached to it.[33]

Ironically, Godard himself was in no better a situation financially than his producer. As Truffaut remarked: 'The miracle of *Breathless* is that it was made at a time in the life of a man in which normally he would not make a film. One doesn't make a film when one is sad and destitute. […] In the case of *Breathless*, the man who made it was almost a pauper. Therein lies the miracle.'[34] The small budget and Godard's need to work fast, cutting production costs to a minimum, account for a number of technical innovations, such as the choice of real locations, the use of natural lighting and of a hand-held camera, which made the legend of *À bout de souffle* and inspired several generations of independent, avant-garde filmmakers from Europe and the United States. Equally significant in this context was Godard and Truffaut's admiration for the speed of production that characterised low budget B-movie companies such as Monogram Pictures. 'If we used a hand-held camera – Godard explained – it was simply for speed. I couldn't afford to use the usual equipment, which would have added three weeks to the schedule.'[35]

Beauregard imposed Raoul Coutard as the cameraman for *À bout de souffle*, and his choice was to prove crucial to the evolution of the film from shooting script to post-production. Coutard had extensive experience as a photographer in Indo-China and had worked with Beauregard and Schoendoerffer on *La Passe du diable* and filmed in Afghanistan in 1956, as well as on *Ramuntcho* and *Pêcheur d'Islande* (for which Godard wrote the dialogues). Despite his initial reservations, Godard soon realised that Coutard was not only willing but also ideally suited to take on the challenge of shooting a fiction feature as a reportage. Coutard had no difficulties in adapting to Godard's unconventional methods, and went along with the young director's suggestion of using hypersensitive film stock (Ilford HPS and Agfa Record) for night shoots, which up until then had been the preserve of still photographers and documentary filmmakers. A different stock (Gevaert 36) was used for day shooting. However, contrary to the legend that has circulated until recently in specialist circles (up to and including, for instance, Colin MacCabe's biography of Godard [2003]), the Ilford HPS film stock did not actually need to be spliced end to end in rolls of 17.5 metres to make up a sufficient provision for the day's shooting schedule because, as Raoul Coutard testified, they preferred to use whole lengths of film even if it meant timing the take according to the different strips of film:

> If we had 10 meters of film we'd do a take of 20 seconds, for example. We had two or three lengths of 60 meters, that's to say 2 minutes of film, and some of 40 meters which makes 80 seconds of film, and also some lengths of 20 and 10 meters. We bought everything in Paris that Ilford had of that particular film stock. When we had to do a close-up we used a length of 10 meters, 20 seconds, and we had our close-up. The advantage with the Éclair Cameflex is that it's very quick to load, so we loaded magazines with different lengths of film.[36]

The astonishing result of Godard and Coutard's joint experimentation marked yet another technical breakthrough in the New Wave history and paved the way for the long-lasting successful collaboration between the two. Coutard went on to shoot most of Godard's major films, with very few exceptions (*Masculin, féminin, Sauve qui peut, Détective*), for over two decades.

The single most expensive element of production, given the overall economy of means maintained by Godard, was the acquisition of a Hollywood star for the part of Patricia Franchini. Former leading lady in two Otto Preminger films of the 1950s, *Saint Joan* and *Bonjour tristesse* (the adaptation of Sagan's eponymous novel), Jean Seberg stood high in the *Cahiers* critics ranking. She had benefited from an extraordinary worldwide publicity campaign, despite the commercial failure of her previous engagements which seemed to have cast a shadow over her career prospects in the United States. Wanting to extricate herself from the exclusive contract she was under, and helped by her fiancé and future husband, the French-born lawyer, François Moreuil, Seberg managed to persuade Preminger to sell the contract to Columbia. Moreuil, who had met the *Cahiers* team, as an aspiring *cinéphile*, heard that *À bout de souffle* was casting, and had no trouble persuading Beauregard and Godard of the opportunity of hiring Seberg. The contract signed between Beauregard's company, Iberia Films, and Columbia stipulated a very modest sum for a Hollywood actress, $15,000, yet this amounted to one sixth of the entire budget.[37] Seberg's screen persona, coupled with Godard's admiration for both Preminger and Sagan, left an indelible mark on the *mise-en-scène*, acting and narrative of *À bout de souffle*, thus ultimately justifying the significant investment in the female lead:

> For some shots [Godard stated] I referred to scenes I remembered from Preminger, Cuckor, etc. And the character played by Jean Seberg was a continuation of her role in *Bonjour tristesse*. I could have taken the last shot of Preminger's film and started after dissolving to a title, 'Three Years Later'.[38]

Similarly, casting Belmondo as Michel Poiccard can be said to have come as a natural continuation of his title role in *Charlotte et son Jules*. Godard first noticed Belmondo's potential in a particularly scathing review of Marc Allégret's film, *Un drôle de dimanche* [Sunday Encounter], in 1958. Judging the script 'lamentable', Godard greeted Belmondo as 'the Michel Simon and Jules Berry of tomorrow', and added: 'even so this brilliant actor would have to be used differently and elsewhere'.[39] In 1959, before starring in *À bout de souffle*, Belmondo played a young sponger called Lazlo Kovacs, in Chabrol's thriller *À double tour* [Web of Passion]. Godard kept the character's name and used it as Poiccard's alias. Even so, Belmondo's reputation during the 1950s was that of a comedy actor, with a record of successful theatre roles and little experience in the cinema. In 1958, he featured in two light comedies, Allégret's *Sois belle et tais-toi* [Be Beautiful But Shut Up] and Henri Asnier's *Les Copains du dimanche* [Sunday Friends]. The previous year, he acted in Maurice Delbez's *On Foot, on Horse and on Wheels*. In the case of Godard's film, therefore, the interest comes from casting a relative newcomer to the French film industry, considerably younger than Bogart in the title roles that inspired Belmondo's character in

*Breathless*, and apparently better suited to appear in comic capers rather than classic thrillers. Godard, however, invested this virtually unknown actor with the aura of a Hollywood icon through the adoption of one trademark gesture: the thumb slowly going over the actor's lips in a wistful *clin d'œil* to Bogart's screen persona. The final repetition of the same gesture by Jean Seberg visually rounds off the parallel by a symbolic re-casting of the legendary Bogart–Bacall couple as the lovers on the run in *Breathless*.

In a letter sent to Pierre Braunberger during the shooting, Godard measured the extent to which his directorial choices ran counter to the public's expectations, while stretching the possibilities of the film stock and even those of the actors to their limits:

> I would like to be the only person to like this film, I'd like everyone [except Melville and Anne Colette] to detest it. […] Even the film stock, you'll see, will be breathless. Seberg is panicking and wishes she hadn't agreed to do the film. I start shooting with her tomorrow. I'll say goodbye because I must work out what to film tomorrow.[40]

As it turned out, the gamble on technical innovation and the directorial creative control over shooting paid off and *À bout de souffle* marked the end of an era in French filmmaking and the dawn of a new conception of cinema that coincided – as the detailed film analysis will endeavour to show – with the birth of the postmodern *auteur*.

### Notes

1    *Entretien*, in Alain Bergala (ed.), *Jean-Luc Godard par Jean-Luc Godard*, Paris: Éditions de l'Étoile/Cahiers du cinéma, 1985, pp. 10 and 11. (All translations are mine unless otherwise indicated.)

2    Roger Boussinot, *L'Encyclopédie du cinéma*, Paris: Bordas, 1967, p. 86.

3    Colin MacCabe, *Godard: A Portrait of the Artist at 70*, London: Bloomsbury Publishers, 2003, p. 18.

4    Ibid, pp. 44–45.

5    James Monaco, *The New Wave: Truffaut, Godard, Chabrol, Rohmer, Rivette*, New York: Oxford University Press, 1976, p. 9.

6    Alexandre Astruc, 'Du stylo à la caméra et de la caméra au stylo', in *L'Écran français*, No. 144, 30 March 1948, reprinted as *Du stylo à la caméra et de la caméra au stylo*, Paris: L'Archipel, 1992.

7    'Les *Cahiers* rencontrent Godard après ses quatre premiers films', in *Cahiers du cinéma*, No. 138, December 1962, special issue of *Nouvelle Vague*, interview made by Jean Collet, Michel Delahaye, Jean-André Fieschi, André S. Labarthe and Bertrand Tavernier; reprinted in Bergala, op. cit., p. 215.

8    Quoted from *JLG/JLG* in Jean-Luc Godard, *Interviews*, University Press of Mississippi/Jackson, 1998, p. 189.

9    Jean-Luc Godard, 'Montage, mon beau souci', in *Cahiers du cinéma*, No. 65, December 1956; quoted in English from Milne, 1972, pp. 39–40.

10   Ibid., p. 40.

11    Valerie Orpen, *Film Editing: The Art of the Expressive*, London and New York: Wallflower, 2003, p. 126.

12    Jean-Luc Godard, 'Bergmanorama', in *Cahiers du cinéma*, No. 85, July 1958; quoted in English from Milne, 1972, p. 79.

13    Jean-Luc Godard, 'Les Petites filles modèles', in *Les Amis du cinéma*, No. 1, 1952; quoted in English from Milne, op. cit., p. 32.

14    Raoul Coutard, 'La Forme du jour', in *Nouvel Observateur*, 22 September 1965, p. 36.

15    Jean-Luc Godard, 'L'Afrique vous parle de la fin et des moyens. Jean Rouch, *Moi, un noir*', in *Cahiers du cinéma*, No. 94, April 1959; quoted in English from Milne, op. cit., p. 132.

16    Jean-Luc Godard, *Godard par Godard*, p. 215 (interview published in the special *Nouvelle Vague* issue of *Cahiers du cinéma* 138/1962); quoted in English from Milne, op. cit., p. 171.

17    'Jean Rouch raconte à Pierre-André Boutang', in *Jean Rouch*, 4 DVD box set, Paris: Éditions Montparnasse, coll. Le Geste cinématographique, 2005.

18    Cf. Colin MacCabe, op. cit., p. 84.

19    A phrase in the credits of this film acknowledges Rohmer and Godard's willingness to include 'this sketch in the "Charlotte and Véronique" series'. *Charlotte et son steak* was shot in 1951 but only dubbed a decade later (when Anna Karina's and Stéphane Audran's voices were used for the two female characters). The story follows Walter's attempts to make his girlfriend, Charlotte, jealous by introducing her to another young woman, Clara. Filmed in black and white in the snow-covered *décor* of a Swiss village, the film derives much of its interest from the use of lighting, contrast photography and outdoor (deserted) locations to create an eerie atmosphere at times.

20    Pierre Braunberger, *Cinémamémoire*, with a preface by Jean-Luc Godard, Paris: Centre Georges Pompidou/Centre national de la cinématographie, 1987, p. 166.

21    MacCabe, op. cit., p. 21.

22    Interview with Truffaut in Jean Collet, *Jean-Luc Godard: An Investigation into His Films and Philosophy*, translated by Ciba Vaughan, New York: Crown Publishers Inc., 1970, p. 170.

23    As Colin MacCabe (op. cit., p. 410, note 5) notes in his filmography of Godard: 'According to Daniela Giuffrida's filmography, the music was added by Pierre Braunberger, borrowing from other films he produced.'

24    Undated letter from Jean-Luc Godard to François Truffaut, archives of Les Films du Carosse, file 'Jean-Luc Godard', quoted in English from Antoine de Becque and Serge Toubiana, *Truffaut. A Biography*, translated by Catherine Temerson, Berkeley/Los Angeles: University of California Press, 1999, p. 151.

25    Godard to Truffaut in Antoine de Baecque and Serge Toubiana, *Truffaut*, trans. by Catherine Temerson, Berkeley/Los Angeles: University of California Press, 2000, p. 151.

26    Joseph H. Lewis, the director of the cult film, *Gun Crazy* (1949), a *film noir* that influenced *À bout de souffle*, made a number of films at Monogram Pictures.

27    Interview with Jean-Luc Godard, published in *Cahiers du cinéma*, No. 138, December 1962; quoted in English from Milne, op. cit., p. 174.

28    Quoted in Jean Collet, *Jean-Luc Godard*, Paris: Seghers, 1963, p. 174; quoted in English in Michel Marie, '"It really makes you sick!": Jean-Luc Godard's *À bout de souffle*', in Susan Hayward and Ginette Vincendeau (eds), *French Film: Texts and Contexts*, London and New York: Routledge, 1990, p. 203.

29    Cf. Michel Marie's account in *À bout de souffle. Jean-Luc Godard*, Paris: Nathan, 1999, p. 18. Chabrol later explicitly stated that he didn't set foot on location during shooting, just as Truffaut 'didn't write a word of the scenario' – quoted in Francis Courtade, *Les Malédictions du cinéma français. Une histoire du cinéma français parlant (1928–1978)*, preface by Raymond Borde, Paris: Éditions Alain Moreau, 1978, p. 273.

30    Chantal de Beauregard, *Georges de Beauregard: Premier sourire de Belmondo … dernier de Bardot*, Paris: Lacour/Colporteur, 1991, p. 70. Quoted in English from MacCabe, op. cit., p. 88.

31    Godard's homage to Georges de Beauregard in *Le Film français*, No. 2003, 21 September 1984; quoted in English in MacCabe, op. cit., p. 109.

32    Ibid.

33    Interview with Pierre Risient in Claude Ventura and Xavier Villetard's documentary, *Chambre 12, Hôtel de Suède: sur les traces de* À bout de souffle, 80 minutes, La Sept/Télé Europe, 1993. Risient's remark also needs to be considered in relation to Beauregard's insistence on Chabrol and Truffaut's formal endorsement of the project, as mentioned above (note 28).

34    Truffaut's statement, quoted in English in Dudley Andrew (ed.), *Breathless: Jean-Luc Godard, Director*, New Brunswick and London: Rutgers University Press, 1990, p. 177.

35    Interview with Jean-Luc Godard, published in *Cahiers du cinéma*, No. 138, special issue 'Nouvelle Vague', 1962, quoted in English from Milne, op. cit., p. 173.

36    Interview with Raoul Coutard, quoted in English in Chris Darke, *Alphaville*, London/New York: I.B.Tauris, 2005, p. 40.

37    Cf. Claude Ventura and Xavier Villetard's documentary, *Chambre 12, Hôtel de Suède: sur les traces de* À bout de souffle, 80 minutes, La Sept/Télé Europe, 1993. Colin MacCabe mentions a smaller sum paid to Columbia for Seberg ($12,000) yet comes to the conclusion that this represented '50 per cent of the film's back end' (op. cit., p. 111).

38    Interview with Jean-Luc Godard, published in *Cahiers du cinéma*, No. 138, special issue 'Nouvelle Vague', 1962, quoted in English from Milne, op. cit., p. 173.

39    Godard's review of *Un Drôle de dimanche*, published in *Arts*, No. 698, 26 November 1958; quoted in English in Milne, op. cit., p. 99.

40    Braunberger, op. cit., p. 183; quoted in English in Marie, 1990, *À bout de souffle* p. 204.

# 2   The Film

## À bout de souffle and the Cinema of the 1950s

By the summer of 1959, Godard was one of the last in the prestigious *Cahiers* team still to direct a feature-length film. His intense activity as a critic, which began in 1950, had consolidated his understanding of shooting skills and techniques and crystallised his preferences for a range of personalities and directorial styles, eventually leading to his direct involvement in filmmaking projects, either as an actor, an editor or writer of dialogues. Yet, as he recalled in his interview with Alain Bergala, Godard 'always wrote after the others, [he] always let the others do things first. Even the films, since Rohmer and Rivette were the first to direct.'[1] For several years Godard remained in the position of an informed observer and his first short films did not completely dispel this impression, although his collaboration with Rohmer and Truffaut on several occasions provided ample proof of the *Cahiers* group's support and appreciation. As early as 1952, Godard had discovered Hitchcock, and was already writing discerning commentaries on the use of *mise-en-scène*, continuity editing and montage in the work of the filmmakers he admired: Renoir, Preminger, Lang, Hawks, Wilder, and Ray. He followed the progress of Rohmer's early film projects (*Les Petites filles modèles*) and enthusiastically greeted Chabrol's and Truffaut's first features. Most significantly, he became passionately interested in Jean Rouch's ethnographic films and unconventional methods, and later wrote rapturous reviews of the documentaries and fictional shorts presented at the Tours Festival by the *cinéastes* in the Left Bank group: Varda, Demy, and Resnais. All these formative encounters would have a decisive impact on Godard's first feature. Yet, in 1959 the young critic and director felt he still had to make his mark. In February and March of that year, two of Chabrol's films were released (*Le Beau Serge* and *Les Cousins*), and the shooting of *À double tour* (starring Belmondo) started in July. Despite the lack of adequate funding, Rivette was working on *Paris nous appartient*, and Rohmer began shooting *Le Signe du lion*. The real breakthrough for the *Nouvelle Vague* (which got its label in 1957 from a series of opinion polls on generational attitudes commissioned by the magazine *L'Express*) came with the premiere at Cannes of Truffaut's *Les Quatre cents coups*, shortly followed by Resnais's *Hiroshima, mon amour*. Although clearly enthusiastic about Truffaut's success (he was awarded the prize of best director), Godard seemed more impressed with Resnais's film, which for him signalled the end of an era. *À bout de souffle* had to be different, and push the emerging New Wave practice even further into experimental territory:

> I said to myself: we have already had Bresson, we have just had *Hiroshima*, a certain kind of cinema has just drawn to a close, maybe ended, so let's add the finishing touches, let's show that anything goes.[2]

The manner in which Godard set out to highlight the imminent demise of classical cinematic conventions and forge ahead along the lines of the recent film theory at *Cahiers* was going to determine his entire career over the next forty-odd years. Like any *cinéphile* of his generation, Godard was acutely aware of the place that the new filmmakers occupied in relation to the history of cinema that preceded their coming of age. However, unlike the other young directors, Godard's idiosyncratic determination in using his knowledge of film history as an explicit personal means of expression, engrained in the visual and contextual fabric of his first feature, went a step further than Chabrol, Rohmer, Truffaut and even Resnais's recent experimentation. Built on the pattern of a classic thriller, *À bout de souffle* established a complicated and sustained web of cinematic references, whose meta-textual function anticipated Godard's systematic use of citations throughout his later work:

> Our first films were all *films de cinéphile* – the work of film enthusiasts. One can make use of what one has already seen in the cinema to make deliberate references. This was true of me in particular. I thought in terms of purely cinematographic attitudes.[3]

Within Godard's understanding of a historical and synchronic system of reference, directors such as Howard Hawks, Nicholas Ray and Alfred Hitchcock were no longer to be taken as mere landmark moments in the evolution of film genre, in the same way in which the grammar of the early silent cinema no longer merely represented an outdated model and forgotten predecessor of recent technical innovations. In true postmodern fashion, at a time when within the French filmmaking industry some were beginning to embrace its modernist credentials (if one thinks of the *Nouvelle Vague* as the emblematic modernist movement of the period), Godard set out to provide not just his version of the thriller, but also his account of the history of cinema:

> What I wanted was to take a conventional story, and remake, but differently, everything the cinema had done. I also wanted to give the feeling that the techniques of film-making had just been discovered or experienced for the first time.[4]

Moving on from the *politique des auteurs* elaborated by Bazin, and supported by the team at *Cahiers*, Godard developed his own deconstructive method of working with existing conventions in order to expose and subvert the limitations of both genre and filming technique. It is to a certain extent paradoxical, as Colin MacCabe observed, that the theory of the *auteur* in French cinema gathered momentum just as the notion of the subject (and, implicitly, that of the author) was coming under consistent attack from Barthes, Lacan and Althusser. However, one must remember that the most important contribution of the *Cahiers* school of film theory and criticism, and the point over which it fought its battle against the so-called *cinéma de qualité* (the classic French cinema), consisted in elevating film to the status of art, and placing the *auteur* on a par with consecrated writers such as Gide, Aragon and Moravia. It is from this standpoint that, on hearing Truffaut had been chosen to represent France at the Cannes Festival in 1959, Godard raised his voice in the name of 'those [...] who waged [...] the battle for the film *auteur*' and triumphantly declared: 'Today, victory is ours'.

> We won the day in having it acknowledged in principle that a film by Hitchcock, for example, is as important as a book by Aragon. Film *auteurs*, thanks to us, have finally entered the history of art.[5]

But the *politique des auteurs* also needs to be understood in the context of Godard's and the *Cahiers* group's interest in the techniques, style and specificity of cinematic language – a range of concerns that was actually very close to what Barthes and the Structuralist school of criticism designated as *écriture*. To Godard, writing about cinema was already making films, and Astruc's article which heralded the 'new age of cinema, the age of the *caméra-stylo*' laid the foundation for an unprecedented exploration of the evolving medium as *language*. 'By language' – Astruc said – 'I mean a form in which and by which an artist can express his thoughts, however abstract they may be, or translate his obsessions exactly as he does in a contemporary essay or novel'.[6] In taking this statement to its ultimate conclusions, Godard went beyond the modernist stance of the *auteur*, by exploring the historical and synchronic dimensions of film language, and turning it into the stage where the confrontation between past and present, personal expression and existing conventions would constantly be played out and more often than not foregrounded at the expense of classical narrative, continuity editing or any other means by which the filmmaker traditionally suspends the viewer's disbelief in the fictional world of the screen.

## Narrative, Montage and Length of Sequences

### A Story Without a Theme

Inspired by a sensational newspaper story and purporting to respect the conventions of the low-budget thriller, *À bout de souffle* displays a fairly classical narrative structure at first sight. The unity of the action that takes place over three days and two nights matches the linear unfolding of events: Michel Poiccard leaves Marseille on a Friday morning, he arrives in Paris early on Saturday, goes to see his ex-girlfriend (the continuity person) at seven thirty, later meets Patricia on the Champs-Élysées, they part and he spends the night alone in her hotel room, where she finds him on Sunday morning. As the police investigation closes in on them, Michel and Patricia look for Berruti and eventually meet up with him at Montparnasse on Sunday evening. They spend their last night together in the Swedish photographer's studio and Michel is shot down by the police the next morning, following Patricia's early call. 'What time is it?' Michel asks her, when she returns to the flat after having spoken to the police. 'Five o'clock' Patricia replies. On several occasions throughout the film, temporal cues intervene with surprising, almost emphatic, precision, punctuating every step of the action. Michel constantly asks the time, and the fast pace of editing during certain sequences or even within the same shot highlights not only the character's race against the clock, but also the film's overall deployment of the action-thriller narrative conventions. Explicitly coupled to the protagonist's obsession with time is the recurrent thematic postulation of death and impossible love, a recognisable leitmotif in all Godard's later work, with very few exceptions. Three years after completing *À bout de souffle*, Godard curiously remarked on the lack of a unifying theme in his first feature:

> *À bout de souffle* is a story, not a theme. A theme is something simple and vast which can be summed up in twenty seconds: vengeance, pleasure. A story takes twenty minutes to sum up. *Le Petit Soldat* has a theme: a young man is mixed up, realizes this, and tries to find clarity. In *Une femme est une femme*, a girl wants a baby right away. In *À bout de souffle* I was looking for the theme right through the shooting, and finally became interested in Belmondo. I saw him as a sort of block to be filmed to discover what lay inside. Seberg, on the other hand, was an actress whom I wanted to see doing little things which amused me: this was the *cinéphile* side of me, which no longer exists.[7]

However, even before shooting began, and therefore before Godard's relationship with his actors could have any impact on the continuity script, the young director had no apparent difficulty in identifying the theme of his film when he wrote to Truffaut in August 1959: 'Roughly speaking, the subject will be the story of a boy who thinks of death and of a girl who doesn't.'[8] Despite the ambiguous phrasing which seems to collapse Godard's notions of 'story' and 'subject' [*sujet*, in French], the remark made in 1959 contrasts with the later assessment of *À bout de souffle*, as a film without a theme [*sujet*], and points to a significant development in the filmmaker's understanding of narrative construction that requires further critical investigation. According to all witness accounts, including Godard's own statements, *À bout de souffle* was shot without a written continuity script, and the actual sequences and dialogues evolved from one day to the next, throughout the four weeks of shooting, more often than not without clear planning, although the broad narrative lines and the psychology of the characters had been established beforehand (based, as one may surmise, on the scenario that Godard and Truffaut had submitted to the producer). Godard described his method in terms of 'last-minute focusing' rather than sheer improvisation:

> My first shorts were prepared very carefully and shot very quickly. *À bout de souffle* began this way. I had written the first scene (Jean Seberg on the Champs-Élysées), and for the rest I had a pile of notes for each scene. I said to myself, this is terrible. I stopped everything. Then I thought: in a single day, if one knows how to go about it, one should be able to complete a dozen takes. Only instead of planning ahead, I shall invent at the last minute. If you know where you're going it ought to be possible. This isn't improvisation but last-minute focusing.[9]

For instance, the third sequence which depicts Poiccard's arrival in Paris early in the morning after the shooting on the Nationale 7, features little dialogue at first and relies on fairly swift continuity editing to further the story, despite the unusually sedate opening shot tracking left to right along the streets of Paris, with Notre Dame cathedral coming into view as an establishing landmark. The slow and almost melancholy score that accompanies this extreme long shot of the Parisian cityscape filmed from inside a car further underlines the sudden transition and temporal lapse between the scenes, in sharp contrast to the dramatic jazz trumpet and drums score which accompanied Poiccard's frantic

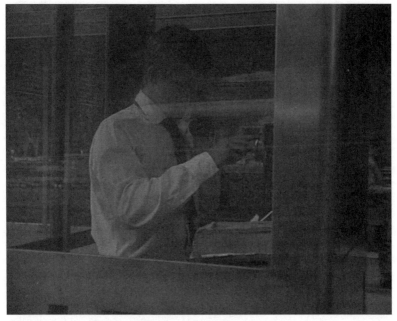

Michel goes into a phone booth (first day of shooting)

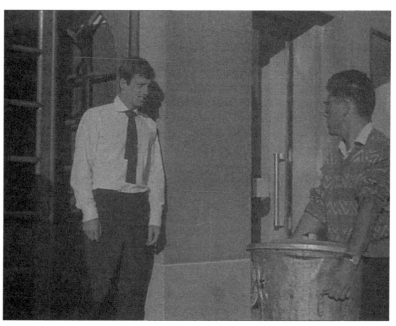

Michel coming out of a hotel doorway (sequence 3)

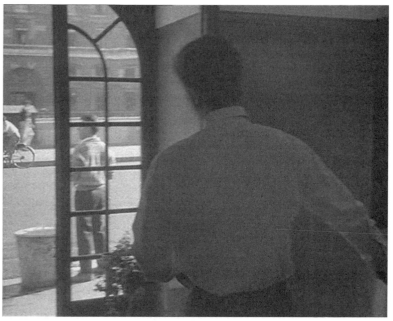

180° change of camera angle (Michel inside the hotel)

run across the fields in the preceding shot. As we see Michel in the back seat of a 2CV car pulling into frame in pastiche, B-movie fashion, his musical theme returns. The next medium-long shot tracks Michel left to right as he goes into a phone booth, deposits a coin, decides not to make the call and gets frustrated when he cannot retrieve his coin. As Belmondo recalled, this particular scene was completed on the first day of shooting, near the Notre-Dame café, when Godard asked him to go into the telephone booth across the street, and told him: '"Well, say what you want". Then: "I have no other ideas, this is it for today".' According to Belmondo, working with Godard was a 'complete liberation' from the acting canon he had been accustomed with in the theatre and in his previous filming career. However, 'Beauregard, the producer, was furiously angry'.[10] The manner in which the sequence was finally edited also illustrates Godard's working methods and sparing narrative style. Two short scenes follow after the phone booth shot: Michel buys a newspaper from a man on a bicycle and begins to read it as he walks, obviously looking for news of the crime on the Nationale 7. Next he is seen coming out of a hotel doorway and asking the receptionist about Patricia Franchini's room number only to be told that she no longer lives there. A swift cut accompanied by a 180° change of camera angle shows Poiccard inside the hotel at the reception desk anxiously checking that the receptionist is still on the pavement, with his back turned to the door. Poiccard then gets a key from behind the desk and walks to the staircase (right of the frame) only to be seen coming out of a bathroom, and facing the camera, in the next shot. The camera tracks him left to right and back again as he goes to check the drawer of a bedside table and remarks in passing: 'Girls never have a penny!' The length of individual shots in the sequence so far varies from a couple of seconds to around ten seconds for the brief visit to Patricia's hotel room, the continuity across one cut being ensured by the playful jazz music on the soundtrack. As the music ends, the change of location is accompanied by the transition to what seems like the real sound environment of a café, with Poiccard's voice and surrounding noise of cutlery and background conversation on the same level. A medium-long shot of Poiccard at the counter ordering a beer then turning around to look for change in his pocket is followed by a close-up of his outstretched hand with a few coins that he counts as we hear him ask the price of ham and eggs and the waitress replying that it is one franc and eighty centimes, clearly more than he can afford. Another quick cut to a medium shot of Poiccard turning to the counter and agreeing to order reveals a 180° change of the camera angle coupled with a tracking movement right to left as he announces that he is going out to buy a paper and leaves without paying. The realistic, spontaneous unfolding of the scene is enhanced by the flowing movement of the camera that pans inside the café to follow Poiccard through the bay windows while the background conversation and the environmental noise imbue this shot with a distinct documentary feel. Alternating short lateral-panning camera movements with shots of Poiccard coming towards the camera at a perpendicular angle compared to his previous spatial orientation in the frame becomes a visual motif at this point which links

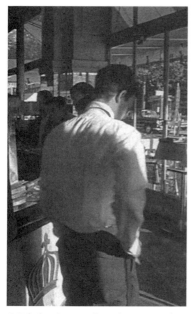 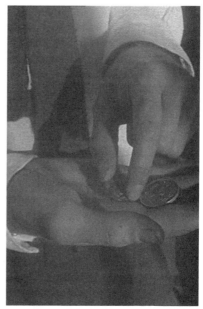

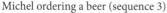

Michel ordering a beer (sequence 3)    Close-up of his outstretched hand with a few coins

his visit to Patricia's hotel to his other call on an ex-girlfriend. We see Michel running through a passage into a courtyard with an open newspaper in his hand. When he is in mid shot, coming out of the archway, he turns left of the screen and slows down, leafing through the paper. Piano arpeggios play in the background, suggesting perhaps his return to a more familiar, domestic environment – hence his sudden reflex gesture to put his foot on a railing by a stairway in order to buff his shoes with the paper, before tossing it to the ground and jumping down the stairs. The camera suddenly seems to mirror the protagonist's nonchalant demeanour as it renders Michel's rapid progression up several floors by an extremely brief tilt from the doorway up the side of the building. Thus the cut to the close-up of a young woman's face as she opens the door and greets her visitor with an 'Oh, là, là! Michel!' comes as the climax of a visual crescendo of short staccato scenes leading in a rather haphazard, frantic manner from the phone booth scene and the rush of central Paris to the relative calm of this encounter, in which dialogue will resume its usual narrative prerogative.

Another important aspect that one has to keep in mind when analysing the narrative of *À bout de souffle* is that the film was shot silent, and Godard cued the lines at the last moment. The actors were not expected to improvise the dialogue in keeping with some worked-out narrative or psychological framework, but they had no previous knowledge of the lines they would say in any one take, and therefore had not rehearsed or learned the dialogue:

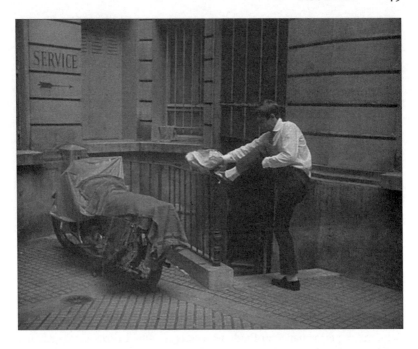

The camera mirrors the protagonist's nonchalant demeanour

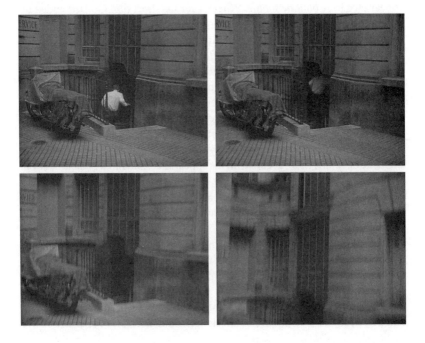

> I read in *Sight and Sound* that I improvised Actors' Studio fashion, with actors to whom one says 'You are so-and-so; take it from there'. But Belmondo never invented his own dialogue. It was written. But the actors didn't learn it: the film was shot silent, and I cued the lines.[11]

Shooting a silent film in real locations with a crew reduced to a minimum, and sometimes with a hidden camera, provided added authenticity and ensured the speed of filming, but – most importantly for Godard's whole approach to his first feature – it allowed for an unprecedented freedom of the actor (and, implicitly, of the director's own input and style). If Godard sometimes relied on the actors' spontaneous reactions, as in the bedroom scene when he asked Seberg to reply to Belmondo's line (cued by Godard): 'All Americans are stupid because they like La Fayette and Maurice Chevalier who are the most stupid of all Frenchmen',[12] the interaction between director and actor yielded results that invariably remained within the former's careful narratorial control:

> My attitude towards [actors] has always been in part that of an interviewer faced by an interviewee. I run behind and ask him something. At the same time, it is I who plan the course. If he gets tired or out of breath, I know he won't say the same as he would in other circumstances. But I have changed him in the way I planned the course.[13]

Belmondo's performance in the hotel sequence is to a certain extent based on his previous role in *Charlotte et son Jules*, acting next to Anne Colette, an actress whose sporty haircut and 1950s-style dress recall Jean Seberg's iconic appearance in *À bout de souffle*. Whereas for his short film Godard ended up dubbing Belmondo's monologue in post-production (because the actor had been drafted for military service in Algeria), a subtler ventriloquism occurs in the hotel sequence in *À bout de souffle*: even if the director cued in the lines the actors clearly had greater independence in delivering the lines as well as dubbing themselves in the end. Belmondo's acting in particular is beguiling though less contrived or 'theatrical' (quite the opposite of his self-referential admission of theatricality in *Charlotte et son Jules*), therefore better adapted to the offhand, streetwise manner of a petty thief on the run. In the first shot of the hotel sequence Belmondo is seen lying in bed like in his previous role, but this time he seems more at ease with his appearance, and has less qualms about displaying his half-naked athletic body, probably as a result of years of amateur boxing (to which he jokingly refers in a quasi-autobiographical remark at the end of the scene when he and Seberg are preparing to go out: 'I'm not especially handsome, but I'm a great boxer'). Poiccard's discourse is peppered with slang and foreign colloquialisms ('Buongiorno!', 'As you like it, baby', 'ciao', 'amigo'), which Belmondo delivers in a convincingly offhand manner, in tune with his stereotyped French verbal puns ('Maintenant, je fonce, Alphonse!', 'Tu parles, Charles!'), and his *cliché* misogynistic remarks ('Women drivers, completely gutless!'). One extraordinary piece of silent acting that both protagonists share and that becomes a distinctive leitmotif in the film consists of a series of three

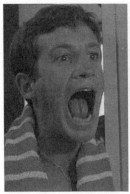 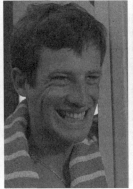 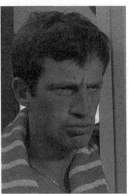

'To be sulking' (idiosyncratic non-verbal bond between characters)

grimaces that Poiccard performs first in order to illustrate the meaning of the phrase 'faire la gueule' [to be sulking] and persuade Patricia that doing so doesn't become her: he opens his mouth wide forming 'ah', then baring his teeth for 'eeh' and finally frowning and pursing his lips for 'mmh'. Patricia imitates him, while looking at herself in the bathroom mirror, only to conclude ironically that this 'suits [her] just fine'. Apart from the allusion to Belmondo's line in *Charlotte et son Jules*: 'Qu'est-ce que c'est faire du cinéma? Une grosse tête en train de faire des grimaces dans une petite salle' [What is cinema? A big head pulling faces in a small theatre hall], the scene establishes an idiosyncratic non-verbal bond between characters that are otherwise constantly plagued by cultural misperceptions and linguistic quid pro quo. Belmondo's unconventional facial traits, his broken nose and big lips not only made Seberg's provocatively androgynous beauty stand out, but also harked back to the iconic Bogart roles in which the American actor's lip scar along with his singular speech pattern, nasal tone, snarls and grin compensated for the absence of customary male Hollywood looks. If Godard's idea of latching on to a legendary American *film noir* figure paid off in terms of developing the self-absorbed and effeminate male chatterbox from *Charlotte et son Jules*, for his part Belmondo professed a deeper identification with another idol of the young generation:

> There are some similarities between the heroes of *À bout de souffle* and *Rebel Without a Cause*. In both cases, the film is about a young rebel who lives on the margins of society. He feels lost, this young man who goes all the way. This type of hero must correspond to the secret aspirations of many youths whose life is sometimes bland, banal, grey, who would like to act tough [...] but don't dare to. These youths see themselves in James Dean and in me – I'm talking about our characters – not as they are but as they dream they could be.[14]

Yet, perfectly conscious of his unattractive boxer's physiognomy, Belmondo then comments on the paradoxical match between his atypical facial appearance and the role he was asked to play:

And here I was with my broken nose, my offhand manner and my bomber jacket. I didn't speak like in a book but like I always did. I think people expected that. I arrived precisely at the end of an era, the end of the bourgeoisie who wanted to ignore reality. I didn't copy the youth of the moment, I was just being myself.[15]

Godard's statement about À bout de souffle as a story without a theme that he developed starting from his interest in Belmondo's presence ('a block to be filmed to discover what lay inside') needs to be interpreted in the context of the director's overall narratorial strategy – including not only acting, but also dialogue, mise-en-scène and eventually post-production processes. Significantly, despite his impression of being involved in 'the true cinéma vérité' during shooting, as well as acting his part 'in the absolute sense of the word', Belmondo declared: 'À bout de souffle is a film which was constructed [composé] by three characters: the two actors and the director'.[16] In discussing Godard's distinction between the 'story' and the apparently absent 'theme' of his first feature, a preliminary terminological clarification is needed in order to refer the authorial avowed manipulation of both narrative and acting to the established notions of fabula and syuzhet that have long proven their worth in film theory and analysis.

### Remaking Everything the Cinema had Done, but Differently

As defined by David Bordwell (1985, p. 49), drawing on the Russian formalists, the fabula (usually translated as 'story') is 'the imaginary construct' that viewers create, 'progressively and retroactively', and which 'embodies the action as chronological, cause-and-effect chain of events', on the basis of 'prototype schemata (identifiable types of persons, actions, locales, etc.), template schemata (principally the 'canonic' story), and procedural schemata (a search for appropriate motivations and relations of causality, time and space)'.[17] The syuzhet '(usually translated as "plot") is the actual arrangement and presentation of the fabula in the film. [...] Logically, syuzhet patterning is independent of the medium; the same syuzhet patterns could be embodied in a novel, a play, or a film'.[18] The third set of components that Bordwell identifies is style, which is medium specific, and designates the film's 'systematic use of cinematic devices' or techniques such as mise-en-scène, cinematography, editing and sound.[19] Bordwell's further definition of narration as 'the process whereby the film's syuzhet and style interact in the course of cueing and channeling the spectator's construction of the fabula',[20] places a special emphasis on the possible stylistic deviations from the syuzhet patterning, and the manner in which such deviations affect the spectator's activity. Most of Godard's early features of the 1960s (and Bordwell mentions Vivre sa vie, Bande à part, Une femme mariée, Pierrot le fou and Masculin, féminin alongside À bout de souffle) already display marked stylistic departures from the film's syuzhet which deliberately disrupt the viewer's attempt to unify the syuzhet/fabula relations along conventional lines. Bordwell devotes a chapter of his study to 'parametric' narration which he describes as the 'style centered', 'permutational' or 'poetic' use of cinematic techniques ('parameters') to create patterns 'distinct from the demands of the *syuzhet* system'.[21] Although he examines at length the impact of Serialism and Structuralism during the 1950s on parametric modes of narration in the cinema, Bordwell concludes that the wide range of filmmakers from different cultures and periods that have employed parametric principles cannot be subsumed to any one school or historically determined movement. He proposes instead an all-embracing notion of cinematic 'modernism' that privileges homogeneity over discrete individual variations or authorial style, and largely overlaps with the already established art-cinema/(classical) Hollywood opposition. The analysis of *À bout de souffle* that I propose to undertake will seek to establish the self-referential and intertextual use of *syuzhet* patterns and filmic techniques as part of a narratorial strategy that properly pertains to postmodernism. Instances of authorial inscription of stylistic deviations from the norm will be interpreted in keeping with the recent re-assessment of postmodern film authorship.

What set Godard's first feature apart from contemporary New Wave releases was not primarily its perceived value as a manifesto, but the fact that the reception only came to confirm the director's explicit intention to effect a stylistic break with tradition. In stating that he 'wanted to take a conventional story, and remake, but differently, everything the cinema had done',[22] Godard consciously placed his method within the range of self-referential narrative techniques well beyond the scope of the established *fabula* and *syuzhet* construction of the American B-movie genre. The first sequence of *À bout de souffle* is oversaturated with cues that display, and at the same time parodically undermine or comment on (in meta-textual fashion), the character, plot and narratorial voice conventions of the genre. The title shot itself, strongly evocative of Welles's *Citizen Kane* (1941) in the austere white lettering on a black background, is preceded by the dedication to Monogram Pictures but not followed by any actual credits. The implied reference to Welles's revolutionary first feature and the overt homage paid to the low-budget American thriller thus leads straight into the narrative and the aesthetic manifesto of *À bout de souffle*.[23]

### *Montage, My Fine Care*: Analysis of the First Sequence

The opening shot shows the *Paris Flirt* newspaper which Michel Poiccard is holding up to conceal his face. Apart from the allusion to the role which the media will play in Poiccard's downfall, the front-page drawing of a woman in underwear framed by cartoon anecdotes anticipates the protagonist's doomed quest for love in a fictitious world governed by schematic and parodic narrative rules. The voice-over that immediately precedes Poiccard's medium close-up shot as he lowers the paper and whispers to himself: 'After all, I'm an idiot.

After all, yes, I must. I must' has been interpreted in terms of a meta-textual inscription of the director's defiant statement of intentions: 'It was absolutely essential that this first attempt should prove to be the work of a master', commented Michel Marie.[24] Other critics have emphasised the physical similarity between the director's cameo appearance in the final sequences of the film and the character: 'Both Michel and Godard are wearing dark glasses. Godard peers out from behind a newspaper (in which he has seen Michel's photograph) as Michel did in the first shot of the film'.[25] Significantly delivered as voice-over, Poiccard's opening line must be coupled with his first rendition of Bogart's gesture of rubbing his lips with the side of his thumb, which the character will later repeat (in shot 93) when confronted with the Hollywood actor's photograph in a cinema display for *The Harder They Fall*. The meta-textual suggestion of a convergence between director and character is thus linked to the 'misplaced' insertion of a character cue that cannot be properly interpreted by the viewer until its recurrence in shot 93. The connection between Poiccard and Bogart's screen persona, however cryptic at this stage, sets off a series of intertextual references – to the American *film noir* and its typical heroes, to Hawks's work of the 1940s and 1950s, to cinematic history and techniques as the wider stylistic context – that are scattered profusely throughout the film, and gradually reveal their parasitical relation to the *syuzhet*, as second-degree narrative markers. What the viewer is gradually led to recognise is not Poiccard's identification with the protagonist of Hawks's *The Harder They Fall*, but the constantly recalled cinematic context that makes his impersonation the copy of a copy, just as his evolution in a mock B-movie thriller plot requires a second-degree reading to detect its parodic and self-referential deployment of filmic conventions.

The editing of the first sequence, depicting Michel's car theft in Marseille aided by a brown-haired female companion, deliberately contradicts the rules of spatial continuity and makes extensive use of '*false* eye-line matches', as Valerie Orpen aptly remarked.[26] Two medium close-up shots, in quick succession, introduce Michel and his accomplice. He looks up, then glances off-screen centre-left, then right. The static shot of the woman shows her looking off-screen right (in the same rather than the opposite direction to Michel, as required by the continuity editing shot/reverse shot rule). She nods, and a foghorn sounds, but despite the repetition of this succession of paired shots and of the aural cue (foghorn), the viewer might be left wondering about the actual connection between the two characters. A medium close shot of a parked Oldsmobile follows, and a middle-aged couple is shown getting out of the car. Cut to Michel glancing quickly to the right, then cut to the dark-haired woman walking behind the couple. She stops, turns and signals while the couple continue to walk. Michel folds his paper and nods in reply to the signal in the next shot. It thus gradually becomes clear that the two spatially disconnected characters are conniving to steal the car, although the conventional establishing shot (including Michel, the woman and the Oldsmobile in the same frame) only occurs at the end of the sequence, along with the first parodic lines of dialogue: 'WOMAN: Michel, take me along. / MICHEL: What

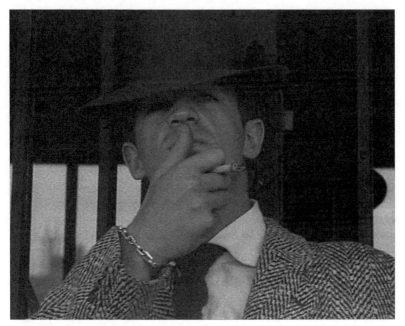

Michel impersonating Bogart (opening sequence)

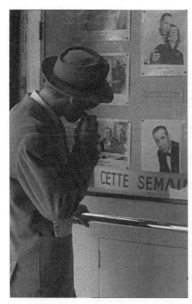
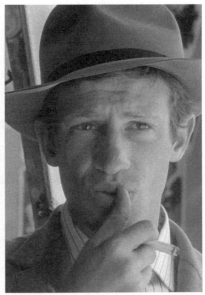

Michel impersonating Bogart (shots 92–93)

time is it? / WOMAN: Ten to eleven. / MICHEL: No. Ciao! Now I'm off [*je fonce*] … Alphonse!' The emphasis on Michel's stereotyped verbal pun ('*Maintenant je fonce, Alphonse!*') sets the tone for the next sequence which playfully disrupts both spatial and temporal continuity, with a disconcerting succession of point of view shots, panning shots, jump cuts and ellipses that are accompanied, on the soundtrack, by a rhythmic alternation of voice-over monologue snippets, blaring car horns, road noise and radio music. Introduced by a dissolve, the Nationale 7 sequence reads as a catalogue of subversive misquotations of classic thriller narrative conventions. Suddenly the *syuzhet* information is coming thick and fast in the form of the protagonist's voice-over monologue, but the viewer's attention is distracted by the proliferation of jump cuts, point of view shots and camera movements which gratuitously fragment the visual flow without any perceptible narrative justification other than Michel's assumed impatience. Consider, for example, the first eight shots during which the rhythmical intonation of Patricia's name, anticipating the exposition of the protagonist's intentions, is interspersed with no less than four jump cuts in quick succession. Starting with the point of view shot of a rural highway seen from the car, and Michel's voice-over singing: 'La, la, la, la … Buenas noches, mi amor', we move on to a middle shot of Michel from the rear seat of the car, as he turns to look at a car following him and utters: 'He'll never pass me in that boat', then turns his head forward again. The next four shots are visually disconcerting, although they lead up to the disclosure of crucial narrative cues:

15. *POV of car ahead.*

MICHEL (*off, singing to himself, **across shots 15–18, cut in quick succession***): Pa… Pa … Papapa … Pa … tricia! Patricia!

16. *POV of a BP oil truck to his right as he passes it.*

17. *POV of a car as he passes.*

18. *POV of an old truck as he speeds past it.*

19. CU: *Michel's right profile. His theme, first heard over the main title, returns.*

20. POV *of the road ahead of him as he passes another car.*

MICHEL: First I'll pick up the dough … (*A car horn sounds*) … then I ask Patricia – yes or no … and then – *buenas noches, mi amor!* (*He begins to sing again.*) Milan, Genoa, Rome. (*He speeds past all traffic.*)

21. QUICK CUT *on blaring horn to LS pan of his car speeding down the left-hand side of a two-lane road. The camera follows from the roadside until the car disappears in the distance.*[27]

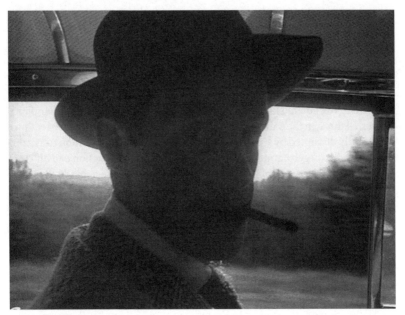

Direct address to the camera

The ensuing succession of shots features an even more disruptive direct address to the camera which blatantly violates the transparency of the classical narrative by drawing attention to the conventions of the medium and thus undercutting the realistic illusion of the film:

23. POV *from the passenger's seat of the passing countryside.*

MICHEL (*off*): I love France!

24. MCU: *Michel's profile. He turns to his right to look straight at the camera and says:*

MICHEL: If you don't like the sea … (*Glances back at the road, then back to the camera.*) … and you don't care for the mountains … (*Glances at the road, then back again*)… and don't like the big city either … (*Glances at road and then into the camera*) … go fuck yourself!

JUMP CUT *and pan to* POV *of the roadside.*[28]

At this point, Michel's discourse serves no obvious narrative purpose. It mockingly interpellates the audience, and breaks the seamless interweaving of *syuzhet* and style that normally helps further the viewer's construction of the *fabula*. Coming after the four jump cuts in shots 15–18, this episode explicitly foregrounds stylistic deviations at the expense of *syuzhet* development. The spectator is thus already alerted to the fact that although the film might be said to have a recognisable storyline that can be reconstructed in keeping with predictable thriller *syuzhet* cues, the narrative contains a second-degree, self-reflexive layer of signification that derives its interest from the playful stylistic exploration of cinematic techniques. One can understand Godard's statement that *À bout de souffle* has a 'story' (or rather, a *syuzhet*) but no 'theme' (no *fabula*), in light of the authorial attempt 'to take a conventional story, and remake, but differently, everything the cinema had done.'[29] From the outset, the classical thriller plot is subverted through the parodic and self-referential re-deployment of conventions. Constantly disrupted by stylistic eccentricities, the viewer's attention to *syuzhet* picks up both diegetic and meta-textual cues for the construction of a different kind of *fabula*. In watching *À bout de souffle* the audience is gradually led to realise that the *fabula* is the process of filming itself, and that the transgressive style guides our comprehension of a postmodern thriller tale, whose hidden story contains the director's aesthetic manifesto: how to remake, but differently, everything that the cinema had done, and give the feeling that the techniques of filmmaking have just been discovered or experienced for the first time.

After Michel's direct address to the camera, the proliferation of jump cuts accompanies the early disclosure of two narrative cues. The first is so fragmentary and apparently haphazard that it becomes almost imperceptible. As Michel changes the station on the radio in shot 27, Georges Brassens's voice is heard singing: 'Il n'y a pas d'amour … [heureux]' [There is no such thing as happy love]. For a French audience, even the truncated line of the famous song would have rapidly evoked the theme of unhappy love, otherwise lost in translation. More significantly though, the next three shots, linked through jump cuts, anticipate the rapid unfolding of events that will seal Michel's fate. His hand goes into the glove compartment, where he finds a gun. Surprised, he exclaims: 'Hey, hey, hey!' Jump cut to his hand on the steering wheel. Michel mimes shooting and makes his own sound effects for the gun: 'Pow! Pow! Pow!' Jump cut to a closer shot of Michel: 'Lovely sunshine.' He points it out of the window on the passenger side and pretends to shoot. Cut to the tops of the trees going by with the sunshine coming through them, and three genuine gunshots call an ominous end to the illusion of Michel's playful sound effects. The symbolism of shooting at the sun bears narrative similarities with Albert Camus's novel *L'Étranger* [The Outsider] and has a cinematic equivalent in Fritz Lang's *The Tiger of Bengal* (1959), as Michel Marie pointed out.[30] The numerous breaks of spatial and temporal continuity in the second half of the sequence ending with the killing of the motorcycle cop (shots 33–49) can be said to find justification in the manner the jump cuts speed up the action and convey a sense of panic. However, the quick succession of long and panning shots leading to the jump cut in shot 37, during which the camera pans right to the front seat and Michel, makes the next couple of shots extremely disconcerting: the image of Michel's car seen from the roadside passing another car from left to right is followed by a quick cut to a shot of the cops in pursuit speeding from right to left (38–39). If the ensuing six shots (40–45), starting with the pan right of Michel's car pulling into a secluded track, display several eye-line matches and sufficient aural pointers to help the viewer's comprehension[31] (e.g. the off-screen sound of the motorbike as Michel looks out of the window to the rear after his alligator clip has broken), the editing of the last four shots (46–49) proves even more disorientating than the previous use of jump cuts in the car chase scene. As Michel walks over to the open window on the passenger's side and reaches into the glove compartment for something we assume to be the gun, an off-screen voice says: 'Don't move or I'll shoot you'. However, instead of cutting to the policeman as the source of the voice, the next image confronts the viewer with a startling 'leap' between shot scales. The cut to an extreme close-up shot panning down from Michel's hat to his

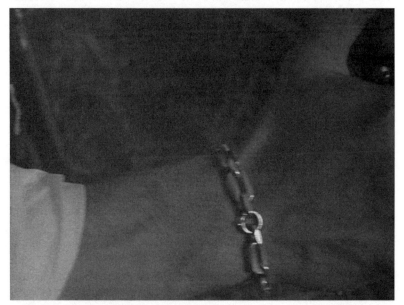

Jump cut to Michel's forearm, wrist and hand

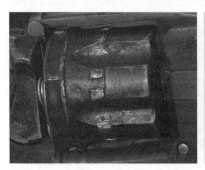
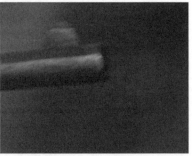

Jump cut to extreme close-up of the gun's chamber panning along the barrel

elbow has more than once confounded the spectator and the occasional critic[32] into believing that Michel was the one issuing the verbal threat. This amazing panning shot in extreme close-up is further fragmented by the insertion of two jump cuts: the first takes us from Michel's elbow to a pan along his forearm, wrist and hand as he pulls back the hammer; the second cuts to an even bigger extreme close-up of the gun's chamber, panning along its barrel. The blaring sound of a gunshot starts on the image of the barrel pointing left to right and finishes, after another 'leap' between shot scales, on the medium-long shot of the policeman falling into the bushes from right to left. The splicing together of two shots displaying opposite directions of movement recalls the use of the same disruptive device in shots 38–39 on the road. But the ambiguity is enhanced by the startling difference in shot scales and the absence of an establishing shot: at no point do we see the policeman, Michel and the car in the same frame (in fact, we no longer see the policeman until he falls backward into the bushes), so there is no way of knowing their position in relation to each other, and any assumptions based on previous eye-line matches and spatial continuity seem contradicted by the conflicting directions of movement and elliptical transitions between shot frames. Is the policeman also pointing a gun at Michel? Has he also had time to fire? The last image of the sequence marks a temporal ellipsis with an extreme long-shot pan across a field at sunset that shows Michel running from right to left on the screen, as the music swells dramatically. It must also be said that none of the previous five shots lasts more than three or four seconds, and the images within the fragmented extreme close-up last only one second, which adds to the impression of a systematic disruption of the viewer's comprehension of narrative codes along conventional continuity lines.

Godard's insertion of successive jump cuts in the extreme close-up has been interpreted as an explicit citation of Eisenstein's montage in *October*,[33] but it is certain that, apart from serving to foreground stylistic deviations and the postmodern intertextuality of *À bout de souffle*, that can sometimes read like a parodically compressed history of cinematic techniques; the function of jump cuts in Godard's first feature remains 'far from being codifiable'.[34] As Godard, the critic, remarked: 'Knowing just how long one can make a scene last is already montage, just as thinking about transitions is part of the problem of shooting'.[35] Despite his declared admiration for classical montage that 'gives the impression of having suppressed all direction', in *À bout de souffle* Godard opted for a strategy that deliberately highlights the filmmaker's intervention at every stage of production and occasionally draws attention to the medium itself. Bordwell aptly commented on the absence of 'a discernible pattern to the jump cuts in *À bout de souffle*' that goes beyond the suggestion of a 'whimsical narrator-filmmaker' to define 'that being's authority principally in the power to sit down at an editing table armed with splicer and cement'.[36] As well as being the first to be amazed by the glaring contradiction between his theoretical views and his practice, Godard also made a significant overall remark about *À bout de souffle* at the time of its first public release: 'I wanted above all to make a film on death'.[37] Alongside other similar reflections on the inherent link between the process of filming and death, this statement opens the way to a possible re-assessment of the strategies of authorial inscription in *À bout de souffle* that takes into consideration both the structuralist postulation of the 'death of the author' and the postmodern exploration of the 'death of cinema'.

### Filming Death at Work: The Postmodern *Auteur*

The narrative of *À bout de souffle* follows in linear, chronological fashion Michel Poiccard's inevitable progression across a series of fateful encounters to his tragic death. However, both the *syuzhet* and the stylistic fabric of the film are saturated with verbal, visual or aural references to cinema that no longer simply foretell the protagonist's demise (by alluding to 'B-movie' thriller conventions) but point to the limits of filmic representation and to the metaphorical 'death of cinema' itself. Amply thematised in Godard's later work – most explicitly in his monumental *Histoire(s) du cinéma* (1988–1998) and in Régis Debray and Pierre Desfons's less well-known documentary, *Vie et mort de l'image* (1995) – the end of cinematic history and the 'death' of the moving image medium as we know it have been a constant concern for the director of *À bout de souffle*. The question of the 'death' or end of cinema (already evoked in the epilogue of *Weekend* [1967], for instance) is neither rhetorical nor merely nostalgic. To the impassioned *cinéaste* of the 1950s who developed a taste for sophisticated citations in his early directorial work, 'death' had nothing of a mannerist and wistful cross-reference, but actually pertained to the essence of cinema and the inherent relationship between film image and time:

> The cinema is the only art which, as Cocteau says (in *Orphée*, I believe) 'films death at work'. Whoever one films is growing older and will die. So one is filming a moment of death at work. Painting is static: the cinema is interesting because it seizes life and the mortal side of life.[38]

This passage from an interview published in *Cahiers du cinéma* in December 1962 concluded Godard's discussion of two directorial styles and two cinematic traditions, the fictional and the documentary, in between which he defined his own approach. Having initially adopted the strategy of documentary filmmakers like Rouch who 'don't know exactly what they are going to do, and search for it', Godard ended up making a feature that, according to his own perhaps overstated account, was more akin to *Alice in Wonderland* than its intended model, Hawks's *Scarface*.[39] In light of his earlier comment on cinema as 'death at work', one can legitimately argue that what evolved during the making of *À bout de souffle* was not the storyline but its meta-textual relationship to a long range of explicitly or implicitly acknowledged prototypes, such as Richard Quine's *Pushover*,[40] Mark Robson's *The Harder They Fall* (1956), starring Humphrey Bogart (cited in the scene which highlights Poiccard's identification with Bogart's screen persona), Bretaigne Windust's *The Enforcer* (1951), also starring Bogart and cited in Poiccard's robbery of a man he knocks out in the toilets and Jean-Pierre Melville's *Bob le flambeur* (Bob the Gambler, 1956), whose eponymous hero is alluded to in Tolmatchoff's conversation with Michel at the Inter-Americana travel agency. Let us also mention Budd Boetticher's *Westbound* (1959), the film that Patricia and Michel go to see when they escape the police, Otto Preminger's *Whirlpool* (1949), evoked on the soundtrack as Patricia goes into the first movie theatre, Robert Aldrich's *10 Seconds to Hell* (1959), whose poster with the caption 'To live dangerously until the end!' we see after Michel's first meeting with Patricia on the Champs-Élysées, and last but not least, Samuel Fuller's *Forty Guns* (1957), rapidly cited in the point of view shot during the bedroom sequence when Patricia looks at Michel through a rolled-up poster. The pastiche of Fuller's shot is all the more explicit as Godard had commented on it in his review of *Forty Guns* published in *Cahiers* in November 1957: 'Eve sells guns. Jokingly, Gene aims at her. The camera takes his place and we see Eve through the barrel of the gun. Track forward until she is framed in close-up by the mouth of the barrel. Next shot: they are in a kiss.'[41]

As the longest scene in the film, which displays a slower pace, lasts twenty-four minutes and features considerably fewer jump cuts than the rest of the film, the hotel sequence during which Fuller's shot from *Forty Guns* is quoted constantly alternates between filmic and literary or pictorial citations. The re-enactment of Fuller's shot is preceded by a close up of Patricia facing the camera, holding the poster with the Renoir painting in her hand, rubbing her eyes and nose as if she has been crying, and announcing that she is going to look at Michel until he stops looking at her. The transition to a more melancholy mood is subtly highlighted by Patricia's musical theme which returns in the background. Their confrontation is rendered as an apparently classical shot/reverse shot, punctuated only by Michel's pastiche gesture, rubbing his lips, followed by Patricia's rolling the poster tighter and holding it to her eye. The next point of view shot reveals Michel as seen through the rolled up poster, while the camera zooms in to an extreme close up and Patricia's theme on the piano turns into Michel's. This suggested aural blending of the their narrative strands is immediately matched by the extreme close up of their lips joined in a kiss, as the camera starts to zoom out until it frames them together by the bathroom doorway. But it is the poster with the reproduction of a painting by Renoir that ensures the continuity with the second part of the sequence, while allowing discerning *cinéastes* to detect a reference to the celebrated French film director, Jean Renoir, author of *La Grande Illusion* (1937) and son of Auguste, the Impressionist painter. The 'illusion' of cinema that Belmondo's character in *Charlotte et son Jules* denounced is once again at the centre of a complex web of references and interconnected visual citations meant to destabilise the realist filmic conventions and passive viewing practices encouraged by the classical Hollywood system. To start with, Patricia wrongly attributes aesthetic quality to a cheap mass-produced reproduction of a famous painting in order to prompt a different response from Michel (PATRICIA: 'You like this poster?' MICHEL: 'Not bad.' PATRICIA: 'Renoir was a very great painter.' MICHEL: 'I said: not bad!'). But almost immediately afterwards, certain details of the *mise-en-scène* (such as the proximity of the poster to the bidet where Patricia washes her feet), coupled with Michel's ironic choice of sensual pleasure over artistic sublimation when he is confronted with the matching profiles of Patricia and of Renoir's painted girl ('I'd like to sleep with you again …') undercut any lofty association between painting and cinema in order to allow for a different set of concerns to emerge, such as Michel's obsession with death and Patricia's anxiety about her possible pregnancy – their next topic of conversation after Renoir.

The astounding range and complexity of intertextual references not only signal a strategy of authorial inscription (i.e. the *cinéaste*'s mark within the existing tradition), but also draw attention to a crucial shift in emphasis from a 'story of a boy who thinks of death and of a girl who doesn't'[42] to a story about the death of 'a certain kind of cinema [that] has just drawn to a close, maybe ended'.[43] Coming just after Bresson's *Pickpocket* and Resnais's *Hiroshima mon amour* (both 1959), the manifesto of *À bout de souffle* had to 'add the finishing touches' and 'show that anything goes'.[44] Self-consciously playing the documentary conventions (location shooting, hand-held camera, natural light, 'last-minute focusing') against established fictional codes of narration, Godard's first feature aimed to expose the inherently hybrid nature of the medium and its fraught relationship to time. Through the palimpsest of filmic citations, *À bout de souffle* points to the imminent closure and demise of the straightforward, realistic narrative relying on conventions of transparency and continuity. The self-conscious acknowledgement and subversion of the thriller plot and character typology makes one aware that Godard's protagonists become, 'to various degrees', 'a sketchy construct, a precipitate out of the mixture of narrational modes'.[45] More obvious still is the arbitrary fragmentation of shots through jump cuts that distinguishes Godard's use of parametric narration from Resnais's or Bresson's editing, which 'however rapid, presents shots complete in themselves'.[46] The idiosyncratic practice of citation, which Godard explains in the interview with *Cahiers* in 1962, does not ultimately lead to a 'polyphony, in which Godard's own voice is drowned out and obliterated behind that of the authors quoted' so that 'the film can no longer be seen as a discourse with a single subject, the filmmaker/*auteur*'.[47] Just as the alternation of continuity editing with the deliberate insertion of spatio-temporal breaks foregrounds the director's control over both diegetic and profilmic events, the web of cinematic references brings into view the author's self-conscious manipulation of narrative codes and identifies him as 'the source of the "open" stylistic texture and *syuzhet* composition'.[48]

The re-emergence of the *auteur* in postmodern film semiotics and practice, after the often proclaimed 'death of the author' within structuralist and deconstructive theories, can thus be said to have been prefigured by Godard's use of authorial inscription that finds support in the recent re-assessment of authorship[49] as a strategy of diversion and displacement of dominant codes in the struggle for supremacy between European art cinema and Hollywood productions. Among the most recurrent postmodern filmic tropes, the direct address to the camera and the author's cameo appearance as a character in his own film have been interpreted in terms of an overt debunking of the essentialist assumptions underlying the modernist presence of the *auteur*, which allows a more self-conscious and sceptical notion to re-surface: the author as builder of cinematic artefacts that re-assemble reality out of a 'compendium of fragmentary multiple fictions'.[50] In the opening sequence of *Annie Hall* (1977), Woody Allen, speaking directly to the camera as both himself and his fictional alter-ego, Alvy Singer, 'deconstructs the very possibility of an author's ability to know and to present some foundational truth about his own or his characters' lives'.[51] In like fashion, Godard's own appearance in *À bout de souffle* as the '*passerby* who reads the newspaper, sees the "wanted poster" on page one, sees Poiccard, and runs to the nearest Keystone Kop to "denounce" him is, in fact, Godard "denouncing" the movie form'.[52] The issue here is not so much the 'death of the author' but the doubling and wilful insertion of the authorial narrative control in a fictional construction that reveals rather than seeks to conceal its articulation.

Godard's foregrounding of the shooting process at the level of *syuzhet* comments on the essence of cinema as 'death at work' in more than one way. The constant interplay between real and diegetic temporality, i.e. the 'mortal side of life' in the process of being filmed and the protagonist's obsession with time and imminent death, is ultimately brought to bear on the materiality of the medium itself. In deliberately going against the seamless blending of lighting techniques and film-stock parameters, Godard was literally pointing at the closure of cinematic representation by stretching the capabilities of the recording material to their limits:

> On Wednesday we shot a scene in full sunlight using Geva 36 film stock. They all think it stinks. My view is that it's fairly amazing. It's the first time that the maximum has been expected from film stock by making it do something it was never intended for. It's as if it was suffering from being pushed to the limit of its possibilities.[53]

Disjunctive montage and the occasional pastiche of 'dated' transitions (dissolves, iris-out) similarly designated more than the shorthand device of eliminating dead time and cutting a film that initially was two and a half hours long. In practical terms, as Godard recalls, some astonishing montage effects resulted from the decision to 'cut between the dialogue' every time 'a discussion between two people became tedious and boring'.[54] However, even when the elimination of superfluous visual material was done 'mathematically' by cutting 'three seconds here, three here, three here' and looking at each shot to see what 'has more energy',[55] the directorial decision prevailed: unlike his predecessors, Godard consistently chose to keep only what *he* liked.[56] This statement interestingly concurs with Godard's explicit parallel between his use of cinematic references and his idiosyncratic taste for literary quotations:

This is much the same sort of thing as my taste for quotation, which I still retain. Why should we be reproached for it? People in life quote as they please, so we have the right to quote as we please. Therefore I show people quoting, *merely making sure that they quote what pleases me*. In the notes I make of anything that might be of use for a film, I will add a quote from Dostoevsky if I like it. Why not? If you want to say something, there is only one solution: say it.[57]

The explicit identification of the author as the source of the intertextual play of cinematic and literary references matches the directorial control over editing and post-synchronisation. Even when Godard famously tossed a coin to decide which of the two interlocutors would be cut in the dialogue between Michel and Patricia as he drives her to her meeting with Van Doude, the idea of cutting between the dialogue while showing only one of the characters resulted from a conscious directorial choice: 'Rather than cutting a little bit of one of them and a little bit of the other, we'll be able to shorten the scene by four minutes by completing eliminating one or the other, and then we'll splice one shot after another as if it was a single take.'[58] Even though Godard worked alongside an editor (Cécile Decugis) and an assistant editor (Lila Herman) the profuse use of jump cuts in this scene, as well as everywhere else in the film, remains unambiguously the director's 'personal signature', as Andrew Sarris observed.[59]

Visual cross-references to early silent cinema (through the insertion of dissolve and iris-shot transitions) also signalled the authorial self-conscious positioning in relation to the history of cinema: 'We were the first *cinéastes* to know that Griffith exists. Even Carné, Delluc, or René Clair, when they made their first films, had no true critical or historical background.'[60] Or, again, in the same interview with *Cahiers*: 'The iris-in showed that one could return to the cinema's sources; the dissolve appeared, just once, as though it had just been invented. If I used no other processes, this was in reaction against a certain kind of film-making; but it should not be made a rule.'[61] Neither a documentary nor a conventional fiction, *À bout de souffle* overtly displayed its value as a manifesto, by playfully designating 'the end of the old Cinema, destroying all the old principles' in the spirit of Picasso's work.[62]

### Soundtrack and Dialogue

Perhaps the most impressive, yet least remarked upon, manner in which Godard's first feature managed to impose its aesthetic break-up with tradition, was the use of sound and music. Many viewers and even the odd film historian[63] nowadays forget that *À bout de souffle* was entirely shot without sound and post-synchronised before Godard proceeded to edit a first version of the film which turned out to be an hour too long.[64] The unprecedented treatment of dialogue and background noise or conversation on equal footing (such as in the café scene immediately after Michel's arrival in Paris or during his first visit at the Inter-Americana agency) gave the impression of direct sound recording, very similar to the newsreel, reportage or *cinéma-vérité* technique. The critical reception of the early New Wave productions hailed the 'authenticity' of the soundtrack that the young directors brought to the screen and, in the midst of the general enthusiasm, the fact that Truffaut's, Rivette's, Astruc's or Godard's first features relied on post-synchronisation was easily overlooked. As Alain Begala's perceptive analysis showed, the light Cameflex that all the New Wave *cinéastes* used for their first films had the advantage of portability but was too noisy to allow for the direct recording of sound. Even if the Nagra tape-recorder, synchronised to a 35mm camera, already existed in 1958, almost two decades passed before the silent, hand-held design of the Arri BL 35 model was introduced in 1972.[65] Interestingly, according to Bergala, the delay in the evolution of the 35mm cameras, from the heavy 1950s model (weighing 80–140lb) to the later portable design, can be attributed to the established production methods of the '*cinéma de qualité*' during the 1940s and 1950s which – given the cumbersome sound equipment prior to the Nagra – privileged shooting in the studio. Technical developments, therefore, did not precede the New Wave innovations – as has often been assumed. In actual fact, the demand for lighter sound cameras arose from the young directors' emphasis on location shooting and enhanced 'authenticity' of the soundtrack and dialogues. After completing his fourth feature (and second film using synchronised sound), Godard was able to say in 1962: 'Broadly speaking the cinema is returning to greater authenticity in dialogue and soundtrack.'[66] Paradoxically, the New Wave's belated acquaintance with the sync-sound recording technique helped to preserve the director's ingenuous approach to the 'realism' of synchronisation that harked back to the miracle of the first talkies: 'The soundtrack is as realistic as possible [in *Vivre sa vie*]. It reminds me of the first talkies, which I have always liked: they have a very real truth because it was the first time one could hear people talking.'[67] Having been one of the last *cinéastes* at *Cahiers* to write or make films, as he recalled, Godard became the first New Wave director to use synchronised sound in 1961, in *Une femme est une femme*.[68] But, as Bergala further commented, the 'equalising' of dialogue and background sound, which blatantly contradicted the classical principle of 'foregrounding' vocal space and made a deep impression on Rivette and the rest of the *Cahiers* group, had already featured in the aesthetic manifesto of *À bout de souffle*.

Working with a hand-held camera but no sync-sound equipment, Godard turned the apparent technical constraints to his advantage by exploiting the untapped potential of two broad categories of post-synchronised 'sound effects'. The first, which relates to the famous 'equalising' of ambient sound and vocal space, mimicked the rawness of the *cinéma-vérité* synchronised shooting and thus reinforced the documentary feel that Raoul Coutard's cinematography (coupled with the use of unconventional film stock) added to the narrative. To a certain extent, this strategy went along with the embedded 'realism' of classical Hollywood norms that had been, from the outset, deliberately mapped onto the sound cinema system. 'The standards canonized by the classical stylistic paradigm' justified synchronised sound, along with other technological advances (such as colour, widescreen, stereophony) 'as progress toward better storytelling, greater realism, and enhanced spectacle'.[69] Except that, in treating parts of his fiction film soundtrack in documentary fashion, without the usual 'sound perspective' (which reduces background noise and foregrounds dialogue), Godard was actually going against the grain, and promoting a different type of aural 'realism' or authenticity. This leads to the second category of sound experimentation in *À bout de souffle* which is by far the most spectacular and can be said to have evolved into a full-blown directorial signature over the years. Shooting a silent film and having to edit the original post-synchronised version down to the standard 90-minute length posed obvious problems that Godard turned into opportunities for exploring the effects of sound/image disjunction. Cutting between dialogue and splicing the shots of only one interlocutor 'as if it was a single take' (during Michel's conversation with Patricia in the car) provides an example of stylistic innovation that helped solve a practical editing problem. Godard tackled the length of the original shot/reverse-shot episode through a succession of jump cuts that introduced a startling visual fragmentation, but ultimately preserved the aural continuity of the scene. Few other instances of sound/image dissociation in *À bout de souffle* seem to be motivated by such practical concerns, and even when asynchrony can be said to further the narrative and speed up the action, the overall strategy is clearly aimed at disrupting classical continuity codes.

Consider the effect of the voice-over that precedes Michel's image in the opening shot and the visual discontinuity that accompanies Michel's voice-over monologue in the car, leading up to the baffling ambiguity between speakers in the off-screen line: 'Don't move or I'll shoot you', followed by the extreme close-up shot panning down from Michel's hat to his elbow. The subtle interweaving of diegetic and extra-diegetic music during the road scene similarly enhances the fragmentation of the image track and the sudden breaks in narrative continuity, such as Michel's direct camera address: 'If you don't like the sea ... and you don't care for the mountains ...' punctuated, at each turn of the phrase, by the ironic insert of typical 1950s radio publicity music. Martial Solal's jazz themes, which otherwise fulfil the conventional function of underpinning narrative continuity, are made to interact with diegetic radio music and other ambient sound in the Nationale 7 sequence. From mere 'leitmotifs' or 'tags that identified characters or situations' in the Hollywood continuity system,[70] musical themes in *À bout de souffle* become set phrases that Godard incorporates into a sophisticated intertextual soundtrack containing both recurrent character or situation cues and meta-narrative references to the authorial manipulation of cultural and cinematic conventions. Recommended to Godard by Melville, for whom he had written the score of *Two Men in Manhattan* (1959), Solal worked with no specific instructions from the young director yet with the clear intention of matching the startling visual innovations of the film. Melville's influence on and cameo appearance in *À bout de souffle* remind one of Godard's playful appropriation of established thriller codes that his iconoclastic filmic syntax constantly unsettles.

More than a parodic rewriting of classical American *film noir* (a practice already apparent in Melville's *Bob le flambeur* (1956), *À bout de souffle* provides the aural equivalent of Welles's *Citizen Kane* in its unprecedented display of an intricate web of cinematic references, highlighted through unusual instances of sound/image disruption. Cinema functions as an overt and recurrent self-referential motif in *À bout de souffle*: posters, star photographs, stills, cinema magazines and film-theatres crop up everywhere with the perfect, if casual, timing of fateful signs and coincidences. Two instances in particular stand out because of Godard's use of asynchrony between soundtrack and image to signal his *cinéphile* allegiances, and thus implicitly situate his first feature within a carefully defined filmmaking context. When Patricia goes into a film-theatre to escape the detective following her, the only dialogue and soundtrack accompanying the sequence are those of Otto Preminger's *Whirlpool* (1949). However, no matching shot of the screen comes to confirm this aural 'citation' of a film Godard admired and mentioned as early as 1952 in his article, 'Defence and Illustration of the classical construction'. Instead, the camera (placed next to the screen) shows the audience and the projector light shining above. Throughout the sequence, from the moment Patricia sits down to the cat and mouse game with the detective, the discrepancy between soundtrack and image conveys a subtle meta-narrative message. On the one hand it effectively evokes the atmosphere of film-theatres in central Paris during the 1940s and early 1950s, a familiar backdrop for Godard's youthful audience, and the breeding ground for the New Wave ideology. On the other, it hints at Preminger's influence on *À bout de souffle* by recalling two of his recent productions starring Jean Seberg. Although *Saint Joan* (1956) and *Bonjour tristesse* (1957) were both commercial flops, Seberg's instantaneous rise to international fame due to an intense publicity campaign made her a particularly fitting choice for the female lead in *À bout de souffle*. More than once Godard acknowledged having deliberately modelled his character on the protagonist of Sagan's novel, which Preminger adapted for the screen.

The second, more sophisticated use of sound/image asynchrony and quotation occurs shortly after Patricia's escape from the theatre where Preminger's *Whirlpool* is showing. No sooner has she joined Michel in the street than Patricia suggests they go to see a western at the Napoléon until nightfall. The next sequence starts with an extreme close up of Patricia and Michel gazing at each other and kissing in the dark theatre, while only the light from the movie screen is flickering on their faces. This time, the soundtrack (music and gunshots) belongs to Budd Boetticher's *Westbound* (1959), as we are later able to ascertain when the two leave the theatre. Nevertheless, the off-screen dialogue, in French, hasn't the faintest connection to Boetticher's film and provides instead an incantatory recital of verses by Aragon and Apollinaire, which sound more like an apt comment on Michel and Patricia's doomed love affair:

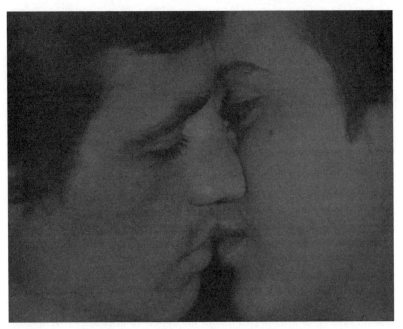

The image consists of an extreme close-up of Michel and Patricia

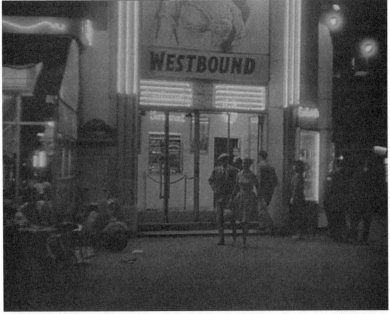

The soundtrack (music and gunshots) belongs to Budd Boetticher's *Westbound* (1959)

MAN'S VOICE: Beware, Jessica / In the crossway of kisses / The years pass too swiftly / Evade, evade, evade / Broken memories.

WOMAN'S VOICE: You're wrong, sheriff … / Our story is noble and tragic / Like the mask of a tyrant / No drama whether chance or magic / No detail that's indifferent / Brings out the pathos of our love.[71] [my translation]

[Méfie-toi, Jessica / Au biseau des baisers / Les ans passent trop vite / Évite, évite, évite / Les souvenirs brisés // Vous faites erreur, Shérif, / Notre histoire est noble et tragique / Comme le masque d'un tyran / Nul drame hasardeux ou magique / Aucun détail indifférent / En rend notre amour pathétique.]

This improbable exchange was not merely intended as a joke on the infelicities of French dubbing of American films, although the obvious clash between the B-western rough jargon and its flowery poetic 'rendition' into French did not elude the critics' attention, and earned Godard credit for one of the earliest examples of postmodern intermeshing of low and high culture.[72] The ingenious collage of two distinct love poems (Aragon's 'Elsa je t'aime' and Apollinaire's 'Cors de chasse') is loosely tied in with the expected 'cowboy' story by the insertion of short prefatory lines meant to identify the off-screen interlocutors as Jessica and the Sheriff. Neither of them, however, appear in Boetticher's *Westbound*, but the substitution of dialogue on the original soundtrack gains added credibility by the treatment of ambient sound and recorded voices, with the same 'shallow, reverberant edge' typical of aural conditions in a movie theatre. As Adrian Martin remarked,[73] the illusion of a single homogeneous sound-space is perfectly reproduced, so that even when we know Godard himself recorded the man's voice (reciting Aragon's poem), this lyrical interlude does not have the appearance of a narrating voice-over or straight authorial intervention which characterises Godard's later productions. Recent critical analyses have therefore tended to move away from a reading of the sound/image discrepancy in terms of an 'authorial signature', on a par with Godard's cameo appearance in the film as the man who informs on Michel. What stands out is the deliberate superimposition of literary and cinematic quotations on the soundtrack to provide meta-narrative cues on plot and character development. Momentarily halted, Patricia and Michel's story becomes a composite fictional construct, placed at the crossroads of cultural codes: the off-screen dialogue of Jessica and the Sheriff echoes the postmodern pastiche of American genre film with a subversive French poetic slant. Godard had a well-known affection for Aragon's quatrain, which he had already quoted twice in his film reviews (first in 1950 with reference to Max Ophuls's *La Ronde*, then less than six months before the shooting of *À bout de souffle* began in a review of Jacques Rozier's *Blue Jeans*).

The treatment of dialogue in the rest of the film illustrates a similar deployment of citation, pastiche and parody as part of a postmodern strategy that privileges colloquial expressions, yet often juxtaposes high and low cultural references and registers of language. Critics have mainly emphasised Godard's originality in bringing 'popular slang and the most trivial spoken French' to the screen for the first time 'since the coming of sound'.[74] Equally memorable, though, is the coexistence of Michel's colourful argotic repertoire (ranging from the pastiche of American B-movie slang, snippets of Italian: 'ciao' or Spanish: 'amigo', to stereotypical wordplay: 'Maintenant je fonce, Alphonse!'), on the one hand, and a proliferation of literary, musical or painterly quotations that punctuate Michel's and Patricia's conversations on the other. At first, during the Nationale 7 sequence, Michel's monologue (which starts off-screen, then is followed by a direct address to the camera) resonates well with the conventions of French cinema *série noire* slang, and provocatively interpellates the viewer: 'Buenas noches, mi amor ... If he thinks he's going to get past me in that bloody car [*sa Frégate à la con*] ...'; 'If you don't like the sea ...' The significant recurrence of verbal as much as visual references to cars in *À bout de souffle* highlights the role that this epitome of speed and male virility plays in the portrayal of modernity. According to John Orr, Godard's first feature, unlike Hollywood productions, managed to capture both the lure of speed and the 'authentically banal experience of the car in the modern age' whereby 'the stolen car replaces the car owned' thus simultaneously displaying and 'denying its glamour'.[75] To a certain extent, through implicit or explicit identification with the cars that he steals and drives, Michel Poiccard himself becomes 'a commodified demon of modernity, a desiring machine, a hyper-active fragment'[76] doomed from the start.

The soundtrack and image of the long middle section in Patricia's hotel room conspicuously blends Michel's Americanese ('As you like it, baby') or his French *cliché* plays on words [*Tu parles, Charles*] with verbal or visual references to Faulkner, Picasso and Renoir. Patricia's quotation from Faulkner's *Wild Palms*, her mention of Dylan Thomas's *Portrait of the Artist as a Young Dog* and the Picasso print on the wall contrast with Michel's streetwise jargon on the phone: 'Hey, kid ... Ciao, kid' [*Salut, fils! ... Ciao, fils*], and his French argotic phrases: 'c'est chiant' [it's crap], 'j'ai plaqué' [I dropped out]. The accumulation of literary and painterly references, reiterated later in the interview sequence at Orly reminds one of Godard's use of the female voice-over monologue in *Une histoire d'eau* (1958) to express his personal aesthetic allegiances. Conversely, Poiccard's colloquial repartees and pastiche identification with Bogart's screen persona undoubtedly testify to the influence of Jean Rouch's *Moi, un noir*, whose post-synchronised voice-over monologue also combined slang expressions with the parodic adoption of American *film noir* actors' names for the young African protagonists. Finally, Godard can be said to have turned the technical limitations within which he was working to his advantage, by using the soundtrack, the musical score and the dialogue to break the continuity of the classical Hollywood system and create a palimpsest of meta-narrative cues and cinematic cross-references without equivalent in the French cinema of the time.

## Location and Cinematography

Apart from the prologue (set in Marseille) and the road sequence on the Nationale 7, Godard's first feature draws heavily on the social and cultural topography of 1950s Paris. Shortly preceded by Truffaut's *Les Quatre cents coups*, in which the city appeared as a protagonist rather than a mere backdrop, *À bout de souffle* ingeniously combined the attributes of a documentary[77] with the atmosphere of a thriller. Contemporary audiences couldn't fail to notice the presence of popular or squalid locations (metro stations, car parks, cheap hotels, cafés, cinemas, dark passageways, junkyards) that were strongly reminiscent of *série noire* films, and echoed the more explicit references to American genre films of the period (Mark Robson's *The Harder They Fall* [1956], Robert Aldrich's *10 Seconds to Hell* [1959]). Similarly, the old harbour in Marseille, where Michel Poiccard performs his first impersonation of Bogart, recalls the Fort de France harbour in *To Have and Have Not* (1944), a classical Bogart–Bacall film, directed by Howard Hawks and set in Martinique.

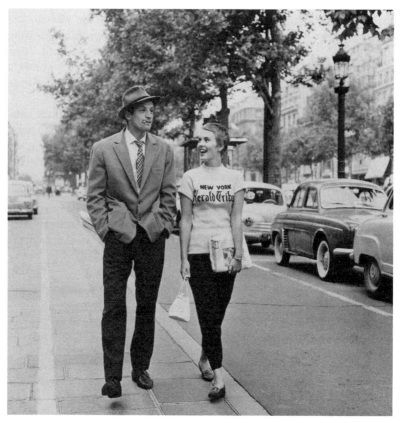

Frenchman Michel meets American Patricia on the Champs-Élysées

On the other hand, film critics and historians had no trouble identifying a thinly disguised evocation of New Wave favourite haunts in À bout de souffle, including the conspicuous choice of the Champs-Élysées (the address of the Cahiers du cinéma's offices at the time) for one of the most memorable early sequences. Setting two further scenes in film theatres such as the Napoléon and the Mac-Mahon, highly emblematic of cinéphile Paris during the post-war period, Godard steps up the self-referential stakes of his pastiche B-movie thriller, with unparalleled postmodern bravado. In meta-narrative terms, the encounter between Frenchman Poiccard and American Patricia on the Champs-Élysées neatly captures the cinematic recasting of Hollywood codes into New Wave jargon that lies at the heart of the film's aesthetic manifesto.

However, apart from the profusion of visual and aural pointers to influential American productions that formed the staple diet of the aspiring filmmakers at Cahiers, Godard's first feature is redolent of another, less remarked upon, cinematic association with Italian Neo-Realism. The impact of Rossellini's Rome, Open City (1945), which Godard repeatedly cited in his film reviews from 1952 onwards, cannot be overstated as far as location and cinematography in À bout de souffle are concerned. Rossellini was among the staunch supporters of the new outdoor location shooting style of filmmaking, whose criticism of the French 'poetic realism' productions and their preference for studio shoot-ing, preceded even Truffaut's scalding attack on the cinéma de qualité (in his groundbreaking article of 1954, 'Une certaine tendance du cinéma français'). As early as 1948, Rossellini declared in L'Écran français that the studio system and the practices associated with it were the great enemy of Realist cinema. A decade later, Godard's contributions to Cahiers du cinéma constantly refer to Rossellini as the yardstick of French Neo-Realism, and the source of the new documentary tradition, closely associated with Jean Rouch's landmark ethnographic films. The preference for outdoor or unusual locations in À bout de souffle (such as Parisian cafés, hotel rooms, cinemas and car parks) therefore needs to be considered not only in terms of a natural reaction to budgetary and timescale restrictions, but also in relation to a conscious aesthetic break with tradition.

No doubt Godard was aware that bypassing the studio system and using a light Cameflex had great practical advantages. Nevertheless, the spontane-ity and raw, documentary feel that came with shooting in real locations, and relying mostly on natural light was something that he deliberately, even obstinately, pursued. Although he initially resented the producer's imposition of Raoul Coutard as the director of photography, Godard suddenly warmed to the idea when he realised that Coutard had no objection to shooting the film in the manner of a reportage.[78] As it turned out, Coutard was ideally suited for identifying the split-second detail that captured reality on the run. He had built his reputation working as a war photographer in Indo-China, and later as Pierre Schoendoerffer's cameraman in difficult regions such as Vietnam and Afghanistan during the 1950s. Most importantly, given his background,

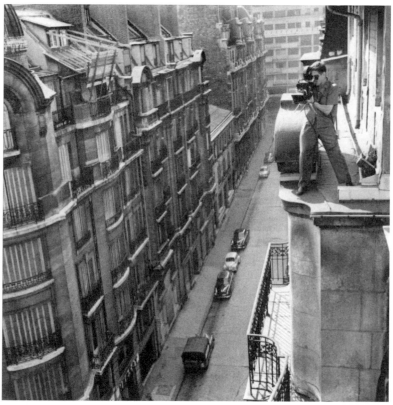

Raoul Coutard during the shooting of *A bout de souffle*

Coutard had first-hand experience of the most light sensitive of stocks, such as the Ilford HPS, which only existed for still photography and which Godard decided, against all odds, to use for the shooting of *À bout de souffle*. Despite the numerous technical difficulties involved in developing the film stock in a photographic, phenidone-based emulsion,[79] the bet paid off and the image of Godard's first feature went down in film history as an example of directorial ingenuity and prowess on a par with Orson Welles's *Citizen Kane*. However one may choose to look at it in retrospect, the analogy owed less to an unpredictable turn of events and more to a calculated effect, given the intended reference to Welles's celebrated directorial debut that looms large over the title score and the first shot in *À bout de souffle*.[80]

According to Pierre Braunberger, 'the New Wave would have never existed without [the Ilford HPS] ultra-sensitive film stock which opened the possibility of shooting in natural surroundings and with less light'.[81] Godard, it must be said, used Gevaert 36 film stock for day shooting, with the same nonchalant self-assurance that was to earn him the unenviable reputation of a dilettante during the three weeks of production, before catapulting him to instantaneous fame soon after the film's release. What others perceived at first as random experimentation and technical blunders corresponded in fact to a deliberate and carefully thought-out subversion of established filming practices. From a sociological point of view, Godard's series of arbitrary decisions (such as interrupting the shooting on the first day when he runs out of ideas, according to Coutard's recollection), firmly establishes his autonomy as an artist in a manner that also manages 'to straddle the contradiction specific to the field of cinema, between cultural legitimacy and cinematographic technicity'.[82]

Having to keep costs down and work fast was certainly an incentive for innovation, but the manner in which Godard set out to overcome existing limitations reveals as much, if not more, about his strategy of aesthetic provocation than about his financial concerns. Writing to Braunberger about the crew's reaction to the rushes of À bout de souffle, Godard admittedly defends his unorthodox approach to filming on grounds of implied cost-efficiency and speed:

> At the rushes, the entire crew, including the cameraman, thought the photography was revolting. Personally I like it. What's important is not that things should be filmed in any particular way, but simply that they should be filmed and be properly in focus.[83]

Godard's further remarks, however, bring into view his differently motivated decision to go against technical parameters and test the endurance of the medium, by pushing it to its limits and thus pointing to the materiality of the cinematic image itself, in unequivocal postmodern fashion:

> On Wednesday we shot a scene in full sunlight using Geva 36 film stock. They all think it stinks. My view is that it's fairly amazing. It's the first time that the maximum has been expected from film stock by making it do something it was never intended for. It's as if it was suffering from being pushed to the limit of its possibilities.[84]

Stripped of its conventional transparency, the cinematography acquires metanarrative signifying status in À bout de souffle, along with the soundtrack, the editing and the dialogues, within a second-degree mock-thriller fable about the end of filmic conventions. The long tracking shot inside the Inter-Americana travel agency in the first part of the film not only illustrates Raoul Coutard's exceptional though unassuming skill as a war journalist wielding a hand-held camera in natural sunlight with little if any preparation, but also brings into view the ingenious use of space and flowing, uninterrupted movement as part of a more dynamic and engaging mise-en-scène at the opposite end of studio productions. Having just witnessed a fatal car accident and having read the news about the policeman killed on the Nationale 7, Poiccard is seen coming into the offices of the travel agency, wearing dark glasses and a felt hat. The camera tracks him frontally in a continuous medium shot that follows a slightly curved path around the central desk to the far end of the entrance hall. Poiccard stops in front of the receptionist to ask where his friend Tolmatchoff is. As he speaks, the camera moves smoothly to his left so that when Poiccard starts going back over his steps in the direction of the door, the camera stays with him in medium shot. The conversation between Poiccard and Tolmatchoff is filmed as part of the same continuous shot that started with Poiccard coming into the travel agency and continues with another track left to right, reversing the earlier movement to the receptionist's desk. A telephone that rings and the conversations in the background reinforce the smooth, natural movement of this long tracking shot that brings us back to the end of the elliptical line of the counter just as Tolmatchoff is coming out to meet Poiccard, his arm around his friend's shoulder, so that without any hesitation or apparent reframing both of them are seen advancing along the same course towards the camera in mid shot. Again, their conversation as they walk along a straight corridor to another office area is rendered with a seamless movement that allows Poiccard and Tolmatchoff to go past the camera as they turn left and follow another elliptical path to a large counter with several clerks behind it. In order to continue filming the progression of the actors without a 180° change in angle, the camera first tracks left (showing Poiccard and Tolmatchoff in profile) then pulls back to a medium-long shot and pauses for a couple of seconds for Tolmatchoff's conversation with the clerk, who hands him an envelope, before starting to track slightly to the right so that when Tolmatchoff and Poiccard turn and walk towards the corridor, the camera is again in front of them. As they come through the glass doors, talking about the cheque that Poiccard cannot cash, we get a glimpse of the modern round office area behind them lit by a set of round neon lights prefiguring the *mise-en-scène* of certain scenes in *Alphaville* (1965), shot once again in black and white by Raoul Coutard. However, the camera continues to track Tolmatchoff and Poiccard's advance towards the main reception desk until a voice calls out for Tolmatchoff from behind the counter and he goes out of frame, left. Poiccard goes once again around the counter to the position nearest to the entrance where Tolmatchoff gives him Berruti's telephone number. As Poiccard prepares to call Berruti from the travel agency, the camera circles around him left to right in order to frame him and Tolmatchoff talking on either side of the counter. This is the point in the narrative when Poiccard implicitly avows to being smitten by Patricia and describes her as 'a New Yorker' – another meta-diegetic reference to the competing American and French cinematic traditions, just as Balducci's character, Tolmatchoff, who works for the 'Inter-Americana' agency can be said to draw on the stereotype of petty crook turned informer of B-series movies. Failing to find Berruti on the phone, Poiccard decides to try elsewhere and says goodbye to Tolmatchoff who responds in their argotic lingo: 'Au revoir, fils' [See you later, kid]; 'Ciao, amigo!' The camera tracks left, following Poiccard slowly going through the glass doors of the agency and into the street, just as Inspector Vital and his assistant enter left of the screen through the same doors. The first cut occurs only at this point, almost two and a half minutes into the most elegantly filmed, if not longest, sequence shots in the film, a tribute to Coutard's smooth and inconspicuous technique of shooting in real-life locations.

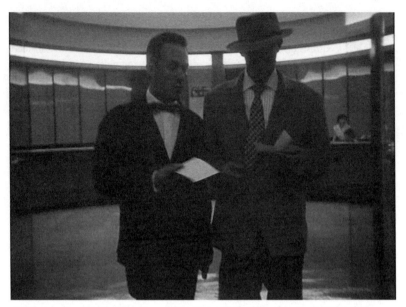

The *mise-en-scène* prefigures scenes in *Alphaville* (1965), also shot by Coutard

To paraphrase Braunberger's remark about the New Wave, it would be fair to say that none of the technical and expressive innovations for which *À bout de souffle* was hailed upon its public release would have been possible had Godard worked in a studio-based environment. Coutard, for instance, recalled the number of highly specialised crew members who usually took part in the shooting, each exercising his authority over the manner in which a given shot had to be framed and lit: 'Before Godard, the cameraman asked for an incredibly long time to prepare the lights for a shot. He demanded no less than two hours for a simple horizontal pan. He could have gone five or six time faster, but he thought: if I ask for less, I exist less. […] He refused certain camera angles and certain movements of the actors, simply to prove he existed.'[85] Similar accounts from Roger Boussinot and Jean Douchet, who worked in the studios, point to the overwhelming power of the director of photography and to the equal influence of the sound-engineer and the art director as part of a tightly regulated activity which went to show that 'the studio dictates a type of [cinematic] writing, a style, an aesthetics in order to better control and disseminate an ideology.'[86] When the *cinéphiles* at the *Cahiers du cinéma* started to make films, the *politique des auteurs* replaced the studio ideology and imposed new production methods, along with more individual directorial styles. 'My main job' – Godard wrote to Braunberger – 'is keeping the crew away from where we're shooting.'[87] The balance of power clearly shifted from the team of technicians and assistants to the director as *auteur* of the film.

Working with a crew reduced to a minimum not only allowed for more creative freedom, but also made it possible to film in crowded outdoor locations in the least conspicuous of manners and thus preserve the authenticity of the scene and the spontaneity of the actors. The absence of the bulky sound recording and lighting equipment meant that the film crew could pass virtually unnoticed in the streets of Paris. One of Godard's ideas for filming with a hidden camera has since become the stuff of cinematic legend: Coutard recalls lying down with the Cameflex in a post-office mail cart while shooting the meeting between Seberg and Belmondo on the Champs-Élysées. For added realism, Godard even placed a few stamped parcels on top of the van.[88] The immediacy of the scene, filmed in a highly evocative location for the *cinéphiles* at the *Cahiers*, captured both the actors' natural reaction to their environment and the lifestyle that went with it: 'You don't live the same way in different settings. We are living on the Champs-Élysées. Well, before *À bout de souffle*, no film showed what it was really like. My characters see it sixty times a day, so I wanted to show them in it. You rarely see the Arc de Triomphe except in American films.'[89] Belmondo's recollection of the shooting in outdoor locations with a hidden camera confirms Godard's instinctive use of documentary filmmaking methods to encourage a more spontaneous acting style:

> First of all, you didn't have everyone around: the technician, the lamp, the stuff […] It was the real *cinéma vérité*. This goes back to the times when I was a student at the Conservatory, and I was acting my parts in the street, for myself […] Nobody paid any attention to us. We talked as we are talking now […] It was a total liberation […] Godard represented a unique moment because I never felt entrapped by the camera, by the technique, by material concerns. The freedom of the shooting was stunning: I never had the impression I was in a film. I was free to do and say what I wanted, go wherever I wanted. Unbelievable![90]

Coutard's hand-held camera also proved to be ideally suited to filming in unusually crammed indoor locations, such as Liliane's tiny room with a sloping roof or Patricia's hotel room, where the protagonists had to climb over the bed to get from the bathroom to the window. The presence on the set was reduced in such cases to Godard, Coutard, the continuity girl and the actors themselves, with no artificial lighting or sync-sound equipment.[91] At times, Godard's resentment of classical continuity rules went as far as to exclude Susanne Faye (the continuity girl) from the shooting, which led to glaring inconsistencies in the actors' costumes, such as Patricia's sudden change from a short-sleeved striped top to a long-sleeved sailor top in consecutive shots during the bedroom sequence. From the point of view of the actresses involved there was something even more alarming than Godard's insistence on striped patterns (among which were Liliane David's striped pyjamas, which harked back to scenes in *Tous les garçons s'appellent Patrick*): his adamant refusal to accept any make-up and studio lighting. However, every twist to the existing shooting practice (including the travelling that Coutard filmed in a wheelchair) was designed to contribute to the subtle blend of documentary and fictional codes, which renewed with the best sources of authenticity in cinema (Jean

Rouch, Rossellini) and pointed the way forward to an *auteur*-driven French film industry.

### Gender and Genre: Women in Godard's Films

As compared to Godard's later productions of the 1960s, gender issues do not immediately seem to occupy the forefront of narrative concerns in *À bout de souffle*. The constant intertextual play of references that the film uses to stake a place within its given cinematic context has led some critics to wonder, for instance, whether the male protagonist is more than a bundle of *clichés*.[92] Michel Poiccard explicitly models his behaviour on Bogart's screen persona and bears all the external attributes of the typical *film noir* outlaw on the run. If his psychology is more complex than this summary association suggests, his appearance points to an unambiguous pastiche of the American gangster-movie dress code: the elegant suit, the hat, the dark sunglasses, to which one may add the character's obsession with fast cars. But reducing Poiccard to a collection of *clichés* and filmic quotations (such as the allusion to *The Harder They Fall* in his mention of boxing) would mean ignoring a whole set of underlying issues that the narrative explores in ways that are very appealing to the audience, yet less ostentatious. Poiccard's story is not so much driven by a straightforward thriller-genre plot as it is inflected and shaped by the imponderable nature of gender relationships. 'What bothers me, right now' – Poiccard admits to Berruti, in the dramatic final scene of the film – 'is that I shouldn't think about her and I can't manage not to.'

Questions of desire, identity, difference and failed communication invariably crop up and threaten to engulf the action, creating moments of narrative stasis. The hotel room sequence, in particular, stands out through its excessive length as compared to the minimal part it plays in furthering the plot. Two other scenes, though considerably shorter, display the same insignificance for the overall progress of events, while concentrating on gender, sexuality, love and betrayal. Patricia's meeting with Van Doude and the interview of the novelist Parvulesco at Orly fulfil the main function within the film's economy: they temporarily suspend the narrative flow to allow a number of underlying concerns to emerge. Significantly, the hotel-room sequence is framed by Patricia's two other encounters (with Van Doude and Parvulesco), which comment on and anticipate the evolution of her relationship to Michel Poiccard, leading to a tragic denouement.

One particular example among many consists of the early hints at Patricia's worries, as yet unbeknown to Michel, but given sufficient prominence in her conversation to Van Doude to alert the viewer to an important narrative cue. The first indication that Patricia's ambivalent attitude to Michel might spring from the anxious prospect of an unwanted pregnancy comes when Van Doude offers her a copy of Faulkner's *The Wild Palms* (the story of a woman who dies after an abortion) and remarks: 'I hope that nothing happens to you like the woman in the book.' On her way back to the hotel the next day, Patricia stops to look at herself in the mirror of a store, and just after a passerby with an infant has walked behind her, out of focus, we see Patricia patting her abdomen and pulling it in, as if checking for early signs of pregnancy. Later, her explicit mention of *The Wild Palms* in her conversation with Michel immediately follows one of Michel's many attempts to make love to her, which she turns down. The reference to Faulkner's novel thus harks back to Michel's offhand reaction to the news she might be pregnant: 'You could have been more careful.' Their different perceptions of the risks and decisions involved in a couple relationship is further emphasised when Patricia quotes the final sentence of Faulkner's novel ('Between grief and nothing I will take grief'), and asks Michel to respond to it: 'And you, what would you choose?' After one final attempt to bring the conversation back to sexual attraction and conventional gender positions ('Show me your toes. A woman's toes are most important'), he eventually replies: 'Grief is idiotic; I'd choose nothingness. It's not any better, but grief is a compromise. You've got to have all or nothing.' Michel's frequent references to gambling ('Now it's double or nothing'), his superstitious slant (when looking for the horoscope in *The New York Herald Tribune*, or crossing himself after a passerby is run over by a car in front of him) suggest an attitude to life as a fast-paced adventure governed by chance, which contrasts with Patricia's law-abiding, bourgeois aspirations.

As one of Godard's early critics remarked, *Alphaville* (1965) and *À bout de souffle* 'have in common the theme of imagination versus logic. Michel trying to get Patricia to Rome is like Lemmy taking Natasha to the Outerlands. Patricia is committed to society and its values: she must work at the Sorbonne, take her chances as a journalist, etc. [...] The challenge to her of Michel's personality resembles the data with which Lemmy confronts Alpha-60; she tries to cope by using logic, and the results are disastrous.'[93] Patricia's attempts at analysing her feelings invariably result in self-contradictory statements: 'I'm afraid because I want you to love me ... And then, I don't know, at the same time, I want you not to love me anymore. I'm very independent, you know.' Michel has no definite convictions or set of values, therefore no need to justify his reactions, which in fact allows him more spontaneity: 'I don't believe in independence, but I'm independent.' To a certain extent, Patricia becomes a victim of her own inflexible reasoning and her predicament is nowhere more apparent than during her conversation with Michel after she has turned him in to the police, as she tries to get to grips with the consequences of an ongoing logical conundrum: 'I don't want to be in love with you. That is why I called the police. I stayed with you because I wanted to be certain that I was in love with you ... or that I wasn't in love with you. And because I am mean to you [...] it proves that I am not in love with you.' The argument is, no doubt, 'lamentable' – as Michel remarks, but the traditional male/female, rational/emotional division seems to be reversed in *À bout de souffle*, as well as in the later *Alphaville*. Incidentally, the two pastiche thrillers also display Godard's ingenious misappropriation of classical B-movie scenarios (such as Fritz Lang's *You Only Live Once* [1937], Nicholas Ray's *They Live By Night* [1949], and Joseph H. Lewis's *Gun Crazy* [1950]) to provide an intimate exploration of gender issues, sexuality and romance within a filmic narrative that acquires, in the first case, the attributes of an 'aesthetic and moral manifesto' of the New Wave.[94]

It is worthwhile noting in this context that the American thriller and *film noir* genre was, generally speaking, a male preserve, with the occasional intervention of leading female characters who acted as temptresses, double agents or objects of desire (if not combinations of such roles), deflecting the protagonist from his course and, in some cases, determining his downfall. To a certain extent, Patricia conforms to the genre codes, while significantly subverting the established cinematic image of 'femininity' at the time of the film's release. One critical comment in particular brings out the astonishment and frustration of a category of viewers expecting the gratification that type-cast roles provided for the male gaze in classical genre productions: 'We are shown a woman who is not a woman but a kind of boy with a shaven head. Belmondo flirts with an anti-woman, which cancels out much of the sexual innuendo that the film led one to expect.'[95] Patricia's provocative mixture of sensuality and adolescent candour, her boyish assertiveness and self-styled elegance (flat pumps and leggings, striped Prisunic dress and dark glasses) owed much to her previous incarnations on the screen as Cécile and Joan of Arc in Otto Preminger's films. The former reference (to Preminger's adaptation of Sagan's novel, *Bonjour tristesse*) is the most prominent from Godard's point of view, which explains not only Patricia's sporting outfits and modern hairstyle, but also the fleeting allusion to Sagan in Parvulesco's interview. The apparently anodyne question: 'Aimez-vous Brahms?' echoes the title of Sagan's 1959 successful novel, which went on to be adapted for the screen by Anatole Litvak in 1960, starring Ingrid Bergman, Yves Montand and Anthony Perkins in a Franco-American romantic drama (obviously reminiscent of Poiccard's transatlantic love affair in *À bout de souffle*). Incidentally, Bergman, whom Godard admired, was the leading actress in Rossellini's *Joan of Arc* (1954), another intertextual hint born out by Patricia's remark during the bedroom scene that she would rather be called Ingrid.[96] The Italian resonance of Patricia's surname calls to mind cinematic associations with the Neo-Realist school and in particular with Rossellini, who became Godard's unwitting interlocutor in an imaginary interview that the young *cinéaste* published only months before the shooting of *À bout de souffle* started in 1959.

Caught between the legendary figure of a saint and the seductive ingénue, Patricia foreshadows the contradictory portrayal of femininity that will haunt most of Godard's 1960s features (*Vivre sa vie*, *Le Mépris*, *Une femme mariée*, *Alphaville*, *Pierrot le fou*, *Masculin, féminin*). In this respect, she is one of the first examples of Godard's cinematic explorations of female/male relationships in contemporary French society. Characters such as Nana in *Vivre sa vie* [It's

My Life, 1962] or Juliette in *Deux ou trois choses que je sais d'elle* [Two or Three Things I Know About Her, 1967] represent, in Godard's view 'the idea that, in order to live in today's Parisian society, one is forced, at every conceivable level, to prostitute oneself in one way or another, or otherwise to live according to laws which mirror those of prostitution'.[97] Although Patricia's role in *À bout de souffle* is not that of a prostitute, her American accent and constant difficulty in grasping the meaning of colloquial French set phrases clearly anticipates Marina Vlady's Juliette in *Deux ou trois choses* as 'typical of Godard's use of actresses of foreign extraction to serve his themes of alienation; the viewer is constantly reminded of French being spoken by non-native speakers, an additional distancing device'.[98] But more than Patricia's accent, her decision to turn Michel in to the police, along with her perceived lack of consistency and motivation, clearly discourage the audience from empathising with her. As Geneviève Sellier observed in her study, *Masculine Singular: French New Wave Cinema*, the viewer is constantly reminded of the 'old stereotype of women incapable of knowing or taking responsibility for their desire'.[99]

Patricia's indecisiveness comes out particularly well in her encounter with Van Doude at the Champs-Élysées café, which alternates French and English as the language of communication and allows one to measure the distance she has travelled since her legendary role as Cécile in Otto Preminger's *Bonjour tristesse*. In the first shot of the scene we see Patricia walk past the tables of a café and towards the camera in the direction of the escalator which is in the foreground. She is wearing a striped T-shirt, a 1950s bell-shaped skirt, flat pumps, white socks and a raincoat. Her costume and subdued demeanour are miles away from Cécile's glamorous lifestyle and carefree enjoyment of life as daughter of affluent Raymond (David Niven) in *Bonjour tristesse*. Playing next to Van Doude rather than David Niven, Seberg seems more sedate, if slightly bored or distracted. However, we can only speculate on the character's psychology and motivation given that the film is mainly narrated from the male protagonist's point of view: it is Michel who delivers the only direct address to the camera and who provides information about himself and Patricia to the audience in a voice-over monologue during the Nationale 7 sequence. The use of flashbacks and voice-over narrative in *Bonjour tristesse* allowed Seberg's character, Cécile, ample opportunity to express and explain her feelings and reactions within the framework of a very conventional screen adaptation of Sagan's novel. Godard's male-centred and iconoclastic take on the Hollywood genre codes such as the *film noir* or the melodrama, afforded the viewer considerably less insight into Patricia's thoughts and intentions.

As she reaches the first step of the escalator on her way to meeting Van Doude, the camera tracks back in a smooth movement and frames her in a middle-long shot going up in the narrow empty space between the illuminated balusters, with an insecure expression on her face, looking left of the screen as her musical theme with trilling flutes returns in the background. This shot, accompanied by the transition from the 'documentary' environmental sound

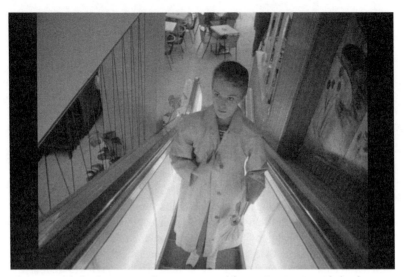

Camera tracks back in a smooth movement and frames Patricia in mid-shot between the illuminated balusters

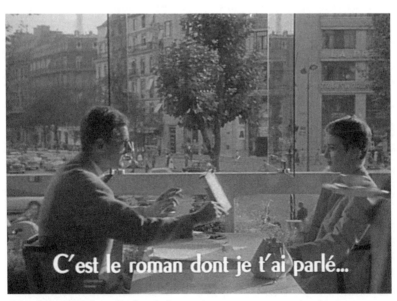

'This is the book I promised to you'

of the café to Patricia's theme, conveys a precious moment of solitude between two encounters after she has just left Michel in the street – a thought signalled by her quick glance back down the stairs just before she reaches the second floor. The image then swiftly cuts to a long shot of the empty restaurant with Patricia entering left of the frame and Van Doude getting up to greet her near a very large window that looks out on the Champs-Élysées. A waiter is seen approaching Van Doude's table from the right and the camera tracks right and circles around until it frames Van Doude and Patricia in middle long shot, as her theme fades in the background. A very abrupt cut, along with a change of camera angle (switching to a middle shot perpendicular to the table) signal Van Doude's dramatic announcement: 'This is the book I promised to you', which starts off the conversation on Faulkner's *The Wild Palms*, abortion and untimely death, anticipating Patricia's still undisclosed worries and her eventual admission to Michel in the hotel-room sequence that she might be pregnant. 'I hope that nothing happens to you like the woman in the book' – Van Doude says to Patricia and further summarises the relevant part of the plot for her. When Van Doude then remarks, this time in French: 'Ce serait très triste si cela vous arrivait' [It would be sad if that happened to you], the camera changes angle and we get a middle shot of Patricia striking a pensive pose with her finger in her mouth (very similar to her reaction to one of Parvulesco's remarks in the Orly sequence), before she quips: 'On verra' [We'll see]. Although she maintains a relatively submissive and passive stance throughout the sequence (as a young female employee hoping to get on in the world would, one may add), Seberg manages this line better than Anne Colette's monosyllabic replies, shoulder shrugging and finger-in-the-mouth reflective moments in response to Belmondo's tirade (dubbed by Godard) in *Charlotte et son Jules*. The camera then stays with Patricia while we hear Van Doude's voice off screen: 'What's wrong?', and Seberg's delivery of the next line, though in rather poor French, comes across as relatively restrained in comparison to her melodramatic performance in *Joan of Arc* or in the final sequence of *Bonjour tristesse*: 'If I could dig a hole in the ground so that no one would see me, I'd do it.' This oblique reference to her love life, together with Van Doude's joking remark about elephants: 'No, you have to do like elephants. When they are sad, or the opposite, they leave. They vanish', once again points forward to the hotel sequence in which Patricia says, after the short love-making shot under the bed-sheets: 'We'll hide like elephants when they're happy.' But it is actually Patricia's next line that seems to hold the key to her psychology in pseudo-existentialist fashion: 'I don't know if I'm unhappy because I'm not free, or if I'm not free because I'm unhappy.' It is not a matter of cowardice, contrary to what Michel repeatedly tells her. It is Patricia's indecisiveness and her uncertainty over her feelings (as she explains to Michel in the final moments in the Swedish photographer's flat) that lead her to turn him in to the police. The story that Van Doude proceeds to tell Patricia in order to 'change her mind' only goes to illustrate the rift between male and female conceptions of friendship and love. On the one hand Van Doude's story sounds glib and is fiendishly fragmented by multiple minute cuts that convey Godard's annoyance with the character as much as Patricia's; but on the other, this innocuous interlude brings into view the power relationships and the exchange of sexual favours for professional advancement that characterised the world of media journalism to which Patricia aspired to belong. The casual manner in which Van Doude tells his story, laughing at his own jokes, attempts to sanitise the idea of sleeping with a 'girl that I've known for years' as part of normal social intercourse. However, Patricia is not taken in and after a short pause just says: 'What's happening to your projects for me to write?', which switches the conversation on to Parvulesco and the Orly interview. But when Van Doude prepares to go and says to Patricia: 'You're coming with me, of course', the only reply she can muster is a mockingly serious 'of course' (reminiscent of Anne Colette's mimicking Belmondo in *Charlotte et son Jules*), followed by two more variations on the same phrase, first in a tender interrogative tone of voice, then brightly and decidedly while he puts his arms around her shoulders. Despite the ironic undertones and a shadow of indecision, Patricia's reaction comes across as a rather facile endorsement of the moral in Van Doude's story about his long-time female friend.

During the bedroom sequence, Patricia's implicit *Bovarisme* – 'I wish we were Romeo and Juliet' – contrasts with Michel's dismissive reaction to highbrow literary references: 'What a girlish idea', and the gender divide appears to be mapped over a cultural clash. Earlier on, Michel mentioned to the script girl that he spent some time in Rome, working as an assistant director in a film at Cinecittà. Conversely, Patricia defines herself as an aspiring writer and tells Michel she will put their story in a novel she is writing. In meta-narrative terms, Patricia cues in most of the literary and painterly references in the film (e.g. the posters or postcard-sized reproductions of works by Picasso, Renoir and Klee, the remarks on Faulkner and Dylan), while Michel's character underpins, in a parodic or pastiche mode, the numerous cinematic associations with *film noir* productions, and with Bogart's star performances in particular. However, as Geneviève Sellier remarked: 'each time that Patricia talks about Renoir, Bach, Faulkner, Dylan Thomas and other figures of high culture, Michel makes a vulgar retort or contradicts her with assurance without her reacting, such that her culture appears more like a social polish than something vital and internalized.'[100]

The dialogue and *mise-en-scène* accurately capture the changing attitudes and the aspirations of the post-war French youth that François Giroud's timely survey for the magazine *L'Express*, entitled *La Nouvelle Vague*, served to highlight in 1958. As Jean-Pierre Esquenazi's study of Godard and the 1960s French society has shown, the lifestyle and daily concerns of the young protagonists in *À bout de souffle* matched the expectations and set of values of most respondents to the survey. Michel Poiccard's restless quest for money was no doubt familiar to a generation who had acquired a taste for consumer goods and leisure activities (travelling, owning a car, listening to music and buying clothes), but who resented the shackles of routine and the 'obligation of earning a living'.[101] Similarly, Patricia's choice of supermarket rather than designer fashion clothes and her and Liliane's use of rented rooms rather than privately owned accommodation reflected the reality of urban life common to the majority of French youths at the time. From the point of view of professional aspirations, being a journalist or a TV script girl were highly rated by the New Wave generation of Giroud's survey,[102] which lent its name to the emerging youthful trend in French cinema. Changing gender roles and differences in the feminine and the masculine views of love, sex and couple relationships find eloquent expression in Patricia's troubled relationship with Michel. While the majority of participants in the survey agreed that love is all-important,[103] the middle-class female respondents rejected the conventional notion of an unconditional or 'absolute' romantic engagement.[104] Even more significant in this context is the overall male insistence on their partner's faithfulness and the 'indispensable' role that physical desire plays in a couple's relationship. Michel's repeated questions ('Sleep with me tonight?', 'You sleep with him?'), suggest a constant, almost obsessive, preoccupation with sex (which he does not distinguish from 'love'), along with inherent feelings of jealousy and insecurity that Patricia's career aspirations stir in him.

In tune with an entire generation of young respondents to Giroud's survey, Godard's fictional novelist Parvulesco significantly places an equality sign between eroticism and love. The Orly interview scene itself functions as a subtle *mise-en-abîme* of the film that highlights underlying gender issues, and comments on Patricia's predicament. Starting with Parvulesco's comment on the difference between American and French women (which echoes Poiccard's earlier remark in the hotel scene: 'I always go for girls who aren't made for me'), the viewer is alerted to the meta-narrative relevance of this interlude for the otherwise 'muted' psychological development of the female protagonist in *À bout de souffle*. Most of the novelist's peremptory statements on love, betrayal, sexual and power relationships between genders seem directly addressed to Patricia, especially following her unsuccessful attempt to place a question ('What is your greatest ambition in life?') which Parvulesco initially declines to answer, as if playing for time. When he argues, for example, that 'between a woman who betrays and a man who abandons, the woman is the more moral', the reflection strikes one as a gloss on the film's doomed love affair, which sheds light on Patricia's inner struggle and exonerates her decision to betray Michel, in similar manner to Van Doude's oblique reference to *The Wild Palms*. However, Parvulesco's condescending reply to Patricia's question about the role of women in modern society makes it clear that he shares Van Doude's mentality and sees women more as a commodity than real interlocutors, implying that a woman's path to success necessarily depends on her good looks or willingness to be seduced: 'Yes, if she is charming, if she has a striped dress, and smoked sunglasses.' The constant exchange of glances between Patricia and Parvulesco, highlighted by the shot/reverse-shot and jump-cut montage of the sequence, builds up the tension to the last two lines of dialogue, which provide the emblematic answer not only to Michel's quest for love and obsession with death, but also to the existential angst of a whole generation that found in the young outlaw's story the French equivalent of *Rebel Without a Cause* (1955):

> 252. MCU: *Patricia looking up from her notebook. JUMP CUT on the same angle.*

> PATRICIA: What is your greatest ambition in life?

> 253. CU: *Parvulesco, staring at Patricia and ignoring all the other questions.*

> 254. MCU: *The photographer shooting pictures.*

> 255. *As in 253. Parvulesco takes off his sunglasses.*

> PARVULESCO (*very deliberately*): To become immortal and then to die.[105]

The final close-up on Patricia's face, staring intently at the camera, prefigures the closing shots of the film and her silent impersonation of Michel (impersonating Bogart's lip-wiping gesture) in an enigmatic superimposition of gender roles and psychological profiles that teases the audience's search for clear-cut moral solutions and challenges the stereotyped *film noir* male/female divide.

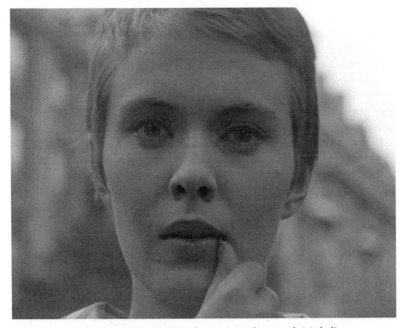

Patricia impersonating Bogart (a sign of secret complicity with Michel)

### A Franco-American Love Affair? Language and Failed Communication

Among the most innovative authorial features in *À bout de souffle*, the use of language and dialogue underscores the symbolic confrontation between French and American cultural codes. On the one hand, the unprecedented recourse to contemporary Parisian slang in the portrayal of the petty-criminal milieu to which Poiccard belongs harks back to the *série noire* films and thus subtly echoes the profuse references to American cinema. On the other, Patricia's imperfect knowledge of French, and her constant failure to pick up on the literal or the performative signals in Michel's discourse, places from the outset the two protagonists on opposite sides of a linguistic and cultural rift that can only grow wider as the film progresses, and which eventually leads to the tragic denouement. Patricia's baffling incomprehension of simple words or toponyms such as 'les Champs' (for the Champs-Élysées) or 'l'horoscope' gradually discloses a deeper inability not simply to grasp but to accept Michel's mindset and values. To his taste for fast-paced living and his obsession with chance, gambling and death, Patricia responds with a need for stability, for social and professional recognition. When Michel asks her to come with him to Rome, Patricia mentions her plans to register at the Sorbonne as the only way of securing her parents' financial support. In the hotel-room sequence she repeatedly asserts her independence by contrasting Michel's casual declaration of love and his sexual advances to the uncertainty of her own feelings ('And me, I don't know yet if I love you'). Although gendered conceptions of love ('girlish' or 'boyish' ideas) are invoked early on in the conversation, the profound disparity between Patricia and Michel, as well as their eventual reconciliation during the bedroom scene, is more often played out at the level of the gaze and of linguistic and cultural differences. Several times Patricia either challenges Michel to a staring game or comments on the impossibility of seeing through each other's appearance: 'I want to know what's behind your face […] I've watched it for ten minutes and I see nothing … nothing … nothing.' It is at this point that Michel resumes his impersonation of Bogart as if to retreat even further behind the pastiche mask of a *film noir* character. Every time it occurs, in fact, the lip-wiping gesture provides a subtle reminder of the meta-narrative meaning of Frenchman Michel's troubled love affair with American Patricia. For their difficulty in expressing their feelings or interpreting each other's reactions only serves to highlight the underlying confrontation between the American and French cinematic codes to which the film constantly alludes. Michel's gestural *clin d'œil* to American genre films does nothing to further the narrative or make him more transparent to Patricia, yet it instantly recalls, on a different level, the array of intertextual references that punctuate the *mise-en-scène*, the dialogue and even the soundtrack in *À bout de souffle* (i.e. from cinema posters and photographs of Bogart to short visual or aural 'citations' and characters' names lifted from popular thrillers). The drama of non-communication acted out between Michel and Patricia at the diegetic level is thus echoed by the meta-diegetic contrast between French and American cinematic conventions. This parallel becomes explicit in the *mise-en-scène* of the hotel sequence which blends the pastiche of quotable American love scenes (such as the close-up in Samuel Fuller's *Forty Guns*) and the jump-cut alternation between medium and panning shots deliberately disrupting the viewer's empathetic, uncritical participation in the events. And as if to dispel any ambiguity over the intended juxtaposition of the star-crossed romance with the divided cinematic allegiance of the film itself, Michel remarks, as he is about to make love to Patricia: 'I'm laughing because this is a truly Franco-American encounter.'

The soundtrack plays an essential part in providing interpretative cues and socio-historical markers that add credibility to the scene and bring out the correspondence between the narrative and meta-narrative layers of meaning. When Patricia and Michel are reconciled and slip under the sheets, a radio presenter announces: 'We momentarily interrupt our broadcast in order to synchronize our transmitter.' The dialogue then picks up the reference to the fleeting identification between the two (as Patricia tells Michel she can see her reflection in his eyes and Michel refers to the 'Franco-American encounter'). Just as Patricia and Michel are getting ready to leave the hotel at the end of the sequence, the news of President Eisenhower's historical visit to France is broadcast on the radio: 'This afternoon, then, President Eisenhower is to accompany General de Gaulle to the Arc de Triomphe, where they will place a wreath on the tomb of the unknown soldier. Then they will go down the Champs-Élysées ...' Indeed, the official parade on the Champs-Élysées, filmed from a high balcony several scenes later, effectively intermingles Patricia's chase trying to dodge the detective through the crowds with the real-life political event. The fictional plot takes precedence over the newsreel framing of the sequence, yet it is undeniable that at all times the authorial strategy in *À bout de souffle* privileges the spontaneity and the contemporary feel of the *mise-en-scène* and the dialogue.

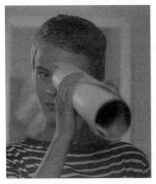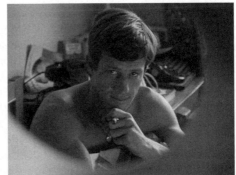

Visual quotation of Samuel Fuller's *Forty Guns* (1957)

The new French cinematic style that the film implicitly sets up against the American model draws on the recent opportunities opened up by ethnologist Jean Rouch's award-winning documentary film, *Moi, un noir*, which had a lasting influence on Godard. The compelling truthfulness of Rouch's portrayal of unemployed youth in the suburbs of Abidjan (Ivory Coast) inspired Godard's similar use of hand-held camera filming, unconventional editing and post-synchronised dialogue. Above all, the powerful screen presence of Rouch's protagonists, whose nicknames ('Edward G. Robinson', 'Eddie Constantine', 'Dorothy Lamour') conjure up improbable associations with the thriller or the *film noir* typology, resonates with Poiccard's impersonation of Bogart and his passion for the cinema. During his brief visit to the script girl's hotel room, Poiccard not only brags about having worked for the Italian Cinecittà Studios but also refers to the unusual display of Lucky Strike cigarette packs on the wall which make up the word 'Pourquoi'. For the *cinéphile* group around Godard, no less than for the discerning general public in France, the word spelled out on the wall was but another hint at Jean Rouch, son of Jules Rouch, the meteorologist and director of the Oceanographic Museum of Monaco, who embarked on Jean-Baptiste Charcot's famous ship *Pourquoi pas?* [Why not?] during the second French Antarctic expedition in 1908–1910. As legendary to the Francophone world as Shackleton was to Anglophone audiences, Charcot and the *Pourquoi pas?* were synonyms of temerity, adventure and discovery that must have appealed to Godard in conveying the pioneering ingenuity of Rouch's documentary and, by the same token, the New Wave's own ambitious exploration of uncharted cinematic territories.

However, the meta-narrative references to the French or the American cinematic traditions were differently perceived, if at all, by audiences with a Francophone or, respectively, Anglo-American background. The 'Pourquoi' hint at Rouch and Charcot, for instance, unsurprisingly left the Anglophone critics searching for a possible tie-in with the rest of the story: 'Michel was an awkward mixture. A hero coming from nowhere; a pattern of questioning, from the POURQUOI spelt out in cigarette packets on a bedroom wall, through all Patricia's questions to the final line; a dead end.'[106] Conversely, not every French spectator would have easily identified the citations of 1940s and 1950s American films that made Kreidl remark that 'the film in fact contains *more* American film iconography and *less* Godard poetry than any of his future features'.[107] Michel and Patricia's drama of incomprehension is interestingly reflected in the uneven accessibility of the meta-narrative discourse that has placed *À bout de souffle* on a par with *Citizen Kane* as one of the first examples of self-referential cinema which 'would not make sense until one knew what it was referring to'.[108]

Two trademark gestures in the film mark the linguistic and cinematic gap between Francophone and Anglophone codes. One is Bogart's idiosyncratic, 'untranslatable' lip-wiping gesture that Poiccard imitates. The other comes up as Michel's rendition of the equally quirky French expression 'faire la gueule' [to be sulking] when Patricia returns to her hotel room in the morning only to find Michel waiting for her. The quick succession of facial expressions that Patricia tries out in the mirror (opening her mouth wide to form 'ah', then baring her teeth for 'eeh' and finally circling her lips for 'ooh') can be said to circulate between them as a kind of private joke or set gestural idiom that marks important moments in the story. In one of the early sequences in the film, Michel pulls faces in the mirror, turning his back to Liliane, his ex-girlfriend, and remaining seemingly absorbed in a kind of interior monologue as she speaks on the phone. Later, he shows Patricia what 'faire la gueule' means and she mimics him while contemplating herself in the bathroom mirror. Finally, her phone call to the police leads to Michel's death and the extraordinary silent exchange between them. As he lies on the ground, Michel looks up at a distressed Patricia, hand on her mouth, and starts making the faces to say 'faire la gueule', which Patricia, unlike the two policemen standing next to her, perfectly understands. The only verbal remark he utters before dying: 'C'est vraiment dégueulasse' [That's really disgusting], is incomprehensible to Patricia who turns to the policemen for an explanation. They are only too happy to oblige and distort Michel's words: 'He said, "You are really *dégueulasse* [a bitch]".' One last time the linguistic barrier prevents communication ('What is *dégueulasse*?'), and allows Patricia to ignore the innuendo, just as she stares into the camera rubbing her thumb over her lip in a sign of secret complicity with Michel that both allows the audience to decode their 'conversation' and denies the viewer any further insights into Patricia's motivation or her feelings when she turns away from the camera so that only the back of her neck fills the screen.

Caught between the pastiche of American *film noir* stars and the new French cinema of outdoor locations, hand-held camera photography and realistic soundtrack that aims to capture the sound and the rhythm of life on the streets of Paris, Michel Poiccard ultimately shares more with Robinson, the character in Rouch's *Moi, un noir*, than with any of his transatlantic counterparts whose example Godard's inadvertent killer on the run apparently emulates. Poiccard's provocative forays into French slang and Parisian argotic expressions bring him very close to Robinson's impromptu voice-over commentary in *Moi, un noir* which Godard enthusiastically remarked on in his film review,[109] and subsequently evoked in the unconventional monologue and direct address to the camera in the Nationale 7 sequence of *À bout de souffle*. As Michel Marie argued, the mixture of Americanese ('As you like it baby') and occasional Italian or Spanish phrases ('ciao', 'buongiorno', 'amigo', 'buenas noches') does not merely make Poiccard's portrayal and that of the youthful petty criminal milieu he frequents more convincing, but also points to the all-pervading 'tragedy of language and the impossibility of communication'.[110] Similarly, the constant switch between French and English in the course of certain scenes (and, most conspicuously, during Patricia's meeting with Van Doude) signals the further intertwining between the diegetic theme of love and failed communication on the one hand, and the meta-diegetic references to different cinematic codes on the other. The audience is thus confronted with both subdued and emphatic hints at a sustained concern with language that affects the dialogue and soundtrack as much as the *mise-en-scène* and the acting, including gestural idioms or 'body language'. Ultimately, the wide range of visual and aural messages that contribute to Godard's sophisticated exploration of verbal and cinematic language becomes inextricably linked to what determines gender differences, power positions and sexual relationships within the film's diegesis. However, the meta-diegetic cues in *À bout de souffle* always bounce off *cliché* narrative markers and the pastiche thriller gradually brings into view a postmodern allegorical tale about the 'Franco-American (cinematic) encounter' running parallel with the provocative exploration of slang, male stereotypes, gender misperceptions, prejudice and lack of communication. More than a second-degree documentary on Seberg and Belmondo,[111] *À bout de souffle* provided, in manifesto style, the first postmodern documentary on the *Cahiers du cinéma*'s aspiring directors at the crossroads between American film culture and the emerging visual syntax of the *Nouvelle Vague*.

## Notes

1    Jean-Luc Godard, interview with Alain Bergala, 12 March 1985, published in *Godard par Godard*, Paris: Éditions de l'Étoile/Cahiers du cinéma, 1985, p. 9. (All translations are mine unless otherwise indicated.)

2    Jean-Luc Godard, interview published in the special *Nouvelle Vague* issue of *Cahiers du cinéma*, No. 138, December 1962; quoted in English in Milne, op. cit., p. 173.

3    Ibid.

4    Ibid.

5    Jean-Luc Godard, 'Debarred Last Year from the Festival Truffaut will Represent France at Cannes with *Les 400 Coups*', *Arts*, No. 719, 22 April 1959; quoted in English from Milne, op. cit., p. 147.

6    Alexandre Astruc, 'The Birth of a New Avant-Garde: La Caméra-Stylo', in *The New Wave. Critical Landmarks*, Ginette Vincendeau and Peter Graham (eds), trans. from *L'Écran français* 144, 30 March 1948; quoted in James Monaco, *The New Wave: Truffaut, Godard, Chabrol, Rohmer, Rivette*, New York: Oxford University Press, 1976, p. 5.

7    Jean-Luc Godard, interview published in the special *Nouvelle Vague* issue of *Cahiers du cinéma*, No. 138, December 1962; quoted in English in Milne, op. cit., p. 175.

8    Cf. Michel Marie, *À bout de souffle. Jean-Luc Godard*, Paris: Nathan, 1999, p. 36. Marie mentions that the undated letter (held in Truffaut's *Archives du Films du Carosse*, and cited by Toubiana and de Baecque on p. 151 of the English edition of their biography of Truffaut) was sent by Godard the day before the shooting began, on 17 August 1959.

9    Jean-Luc Godard, interview published in the special *Nouvelle Vague* issue of *Cahiers du cinéma*, No. 138, December 1962; quoted in English in Milne, op. cit., pp. 172–173.

10   Philippe Durant, *Belmondo*, Lausanne: Pierre-Marcel Favre, 1987, p. 74.

11   Jean-Luc Godard, interview published in the special *Nouvelle Vague* issue of *Cahiers du cinéma*, No. 138, December 1962; quoted in English in Milne, op. cit., p. 173.

12   Philippe Durant, *Belmondo*, op. cit. Belmondo's recollection of the shooting is cited on pp. 73–76.

13   Jean-Luc Godard interview published in the special *Nouvelle Vague* issue of *Cahiers du cinéma* 138, December 1962; quoted in English in Milne, op. cit., p. 177.

14   Durant, op. cit., pp. 75–76.

15    Ibid., p. 77.

16    Ibid., p. 74.

17    David Bordwell, *Narration in the Fiction Film*, London: Methuen, 1985, p. 49. In order to clarify the manner in which I am applying Bordwell's terminology to Godard's remarks on *À bout de souffle* (i.e. a film which has a 'story' but no 'theme'), one needs to remember that Bordwell's use of *fabula* roughly corresponds to what Godard designates by 'theme', while Godard's understanding of 'story' corresponds to Bordwell's *syuzhet*.

18    Ibid., p. 50.

19    Ibid.

20    Ibid., p. 53.

21    Ibid., pp. 274–275.

22    Jean-Luc Godard, interview published in the special *Nouvelle Vague* issue of *Cahiers du cinéma*, No. 138, December 1962; quoted in English in Milne, op. cit., p. 173.

23    In the analysis that follows, the numbering of shots follows that in the continuity script published in Dudley Andrew (ed.), *Breathless*, New Brunswick and London: Rutgers University Press, 1990, pp. 33–146.

24    Michel Marie, *À bout de souffle*, op. cit., p. 201.

25    Charles Barr, '*À bout de souffle*', in Ian Cameron (ed.), *The Films of Jean-Luc Godard*, New York: Praeger Publishers, 1970, p. 11.

26    Valerie Orpen, *Film Editing: The Art of the Expressive*, London and New York: Wallflower Press, 2003, p. 63. The analysis of the first sequence follows Orpen's discussion of visually disconcerting cues, 'false eye-line matches' and spatial discontinuity.

27    Cf. Continuity script in Andrews, op. cit., pp. 34–35.

28    Ibid., p. 35.

29    Jean-Luc Godard, interview published in the special *Nouvelle Vague* issue of *Cahiers du cinéma*, No. 138, December 1962; quoted in English in Milne, op. cit., pp. 175, 173 (see notes 4 & 7 above).

30    Michel Marie, *À bout de souffle. Jean-Luc Godard*, op. cit., p. 84.

31    Cf. Valerie Orpen's analysis of the Route Nationale 7 sequence, op. cit., pp. 64–65.

32    David Sterritt, *The Films of Jean-Luc Godard: Seeing the Invisible*, Cambridge: Cambridge University Press, 1999.

33    Marie, *À bout de souffle. Jean-Luc Godard*, op. cit., p. 69.

34    Orpen, op. cit., p. 71.

35    Jean-Luc Godard, 'Montage, My Fine Care', in Milne, op. cit., p. 40.

36    Bordwell, op. cit., p. 324.

37    'I am for classical montage and yet I've created the least orthodox style of montage.' [...] '*Breathless* is a film about the necessity of *engagement* [...] I wanted above all to make a film on death.' Interview with Jean-Luc Godard, 'I'm not out of breath', in *Arts*, March 1960, trans. by Dudley Andrews, in Andrews, op. cit., pp. 167–168.

38    Ibid., p. 181.

39    Jean-Luc Godard, interview published in the special *Nouvelle Vague* issue of *Cahiers du cinéma*, No. 138, December 1962; quoted in English in Milne, op. cit., p. 175.

40    Ibid.

41    Jean-Luc Godard, 'Forty Guns', in *Cahiers du cinema*, No. 76, December 1957; quoted in English in Milne, op. cit., p. 62.

42    See note 8.

43    See note 2: Jean-Luc Godard, interview published in the special *Nouvelle Vague* issue of *Cahiers du cinéma*, No. 138, December 1962; quoted in English in Milne, op. cit., p. 173.

44    Jean-Luc Godard, interview published in the special *Nouvelle Vague* issue of *Cahiers du cinéma*, No. 138, December 1962; quoted in English in Milne, op. cit., p. 173.

45    Bordwell, op. cit., p. 322.

46    Ibid., p. 328.

47    Peter Wollen, 'Godard and Counter Cinema: *Vent d'est*', in *Readings and Writings: Semiotic Counter-Strategies*, London: Verso, 1982, p. 86.

48    Bordwell, op. cit., p. 324.

49    Rosanna Maule, 'De-Authorizing the Auteur: Postmodern Politics of Interpellation in Contemporary European Cinema', in Cristina Degli-Esposti (ed.), *Postmodernism in the Cinema*, New York and Oxford: Berghahn Books, 1998, p. 121.

50    Marilyn Fabe, 'Film and Postmodernism: Woody Allen's *Annie Hall*', in *Closely Watched Films: An Introduction to the Art of Narrative Film Technique*, Berkley, Los Angeles and London: University of California Press, 2004, p. 190.

51    Ibid., p. 179.

52    John Kreidl, *Jean-Luc Godard*, Boston: Twayne Publishers, 1980, p. 119.

53    Jean-Luc Godard, letter to Pierre Braunberger, in Pierre Braunberger, *Cinémamémoire*, with a preface by Jean-Luc Godard, Paris: Centre Georges Pompidou/CNC, 1987, p. 184.

54    Jean-Luc Godard, interview with *Films and Filming*, September 1961; quoted from Andrew, op. cit., pp. 169–179.

55    Wheeler Winston Dixon, *The Films of Jean-Luc Godard*, Albany: State University of New York Press, 1997, p. 16.

56    Ibid.

57    See note 2: Jean-Luc Godard, interview published in the special *Nouvelle Vague* issue of *Cahiers du cinéma*, No. 138, December 1962; quoted in English in Milne, op. cit., p. 173.

58    Jean-Luc Godard, *Introduction à une véritable histoire du cinéma*, Paris: Éditions Albatros, 1980, p. 34.

59    Andrew Sarris, quoted in Toby Mussman (ed.), *Jean-Luc Godard*, New York: E.P. Dutton, 1968, p. 134.

60    See note 2: Jean-Luc Godard, interview published in the special *Nouvelle Vague* issue of *Cahiers du cinéma*, No. 138, December 1962; quoted in English in Milne, op. cit., p. 172.

61    Ibid., p. 173.

62    Jean-Luc Godard, Interview with *Films and Filming*, September 1961; quoted from Andrew, op. cit., p. 170.

63    Jean-Pierre Jeancolas, *Histoire du cinéma français*, Paris: Éditions du Groupement national des cinémas de recherche, 1993.

64    Marie, *À bout de souffle. Jean-Luc Godard*, op. cit., p. 208.

65    Alain Bergala, 'Techniques de la Nouvelle Vague', in *Cahiers du cinéma* special issue hors série 'Nouvelle Vague, une légende en question', 1998, p. 38.

66    See note 2: Jean-Luc Godard, interview published in the special *Nouvelle Vague* issue of *Cahiers du cinéma*, No. 138, December 1962; quoted in English in Milne, op. cit., p. 185.

67    Ibid.

68    Bergala, op. cit., p. 39.

69    David Bordwell, Janet Staiger and Kristin Thompson, *The Classical Hollywood Cinema. Film Style and Mode of Production to 1960*, London: Routledge, 1985, p. 244.

70    Ibid., p. 303.

71    Cf. continuity script in Andrew, op. cit., pp. 121–152 (n. 55) and Milne, op. cit., pp. 20, 115.

72    Adrian Martin, 'Recital: Three Lyrical Interludes in Godard', in Michael Temple, James S. William and Michael Witt (eds), *Forever Godard*, London: Black Dog Publishing, 2004, p. 262.

73    Ibid., p. 258.

74    Michel, *À bout de souffle*, op. cit., pp. 208–209.

75    John Orr, *Cinema and Modernity*, Cambridge: Polity Press, 1993, p. 134.

76    Ibid., p. 133.

77    Marie, *À bout de souffle*, op. cit., p. 57.

78    MacCabe, op. cit., p. 115.

79    Raoul Coutard, 'La Forme du jour', in *Nouvel Observateur* 22 September 1965, p. 36.

80    Marie, *À bout de souffle*, op. cit., pp. 206–207.

81    Frank Beau, 'L'autodafé du carton-pâte', in *Cahiers du cinéma* special issue hors série 'Nouvelle Vague, une légende en question', 1998, p. 52.

82   Philippe Mary, 'Cinematic Microcosm and Cultural Cosmologies – Elements of a Sociology of the New Wave', in *Cinema Journal*, Vol. 49, No. 4, Summer 2010, p. 164.

83   Pierre Braunberger, op. cit., p. 183; quoted in English in Hayward and Vincendeau, op. cit., pp. 205–206.

84   Ibid., p. 184; quoted in English in Hayward and Vincendeau, op. cit., p. 206.

85   Coutard, art. cit., p. 36.

86   Beau, art. cit, p. 52.

87   Braunberger, op. cit., p. 183; quoted in English in Hayward and Vincendeau, op. cit., p. 206.

88   Raoul Coutard quoted in Xavier Villetard and Claude Ventura, *Chambre 12, Hôtel de Suède: sur les traces de* À bout de souffle, film documentary 1:18':28", Arte, 1995.

89   See note 2: Jean-Luc Godard, interview published in the special *Nouvelle Vague* issue of *Cahiers du cinéma*, No. 138, December 1962; quoted in English in Milne, op. cit., p. 180.

90   Jean-Paul Belmondo quoted in Durant, op. cit., pp. 74–75.

91   Liliane David quoted in Villetard, and Ventura, *Chambre 12, Hôtel de Suède: sur les traces de* À bout de souffle, op. cit.

92   Kreidl, op. cit., p. 103.

93   Charles Barr, 'À bout de souffle' (1969), in Andrews, op. cit., pp. 222–223.

94   Michel Marie, *À bout de souffle*, op. cit., pp. 51–52.

95   Raymond Borde, in "La Nouvelle Vague", *Premier Plan*, Spring 1962, quoted in Marie, *À bout de souffle*, op. cit., p. 101.

96   Marie, *À bout de souffle*, op. cit., p. 111.

97   Jean-Luc Godard, *Deux ou trois choses que je sais d'elle: découpage intégral*, Paris: Éditions du Seuil/Avant-Scène, 1971, p. 12.

98   Catherine Ellen Portuges, 'Cinema and Psych: A Psychoanalytic View of the Representation of Women in Three French Film Directors of the 1960s', PhD thesis, Los Angeles: University of California/Ann Arbor: University Microfilms International, 1982, p. 120.

99   Geneviève Sellier, *Masculin Singula: French New Wave Cinema*, Durham and London: Duke University Press, 2008, p. 115.

100  Ibid., p. 114.

101  Jean-Pierre Esquenazi, *Godard et la société française des années 1960*, Paris: Armand Colin, 2004, p. 87.

102  Ibid., p. 88.

103  Ibid., p. 89.

104  Ibid., p. 90.

105  Cf. continuity script in Andrew, op. cit., pp. 104–105.

106  Charles Barr, 'À bout de souffle' (1969), in Andrew, op. cit., p. 223.

107  Kreidl, op. cit., p. 113.

108  Ibid., p. 118.

109  Jean-Luc Godard, 'Moi, un noir', *Arts* 713 (11 March 1959), in Milne, op. cit., p. 129.

110  Marie, "'It really makes you sick!'": Jean-Luc Godard's À bout de souffle (1959)', op. cit., p. 211.

111  Jean-Luc Godard, interview with Yvonne Baby, in *Le Monde*, 18 March 1960, trans. by Dudley Andrew, in Andrew, op. cit., p. 166.

# 3  Reception and Later Influences

## The French *Citizen Kane*

Contrary to expectations, given its low budget and highly unorthodox editing, *À bout de souffle* did exceptionally well at the box office at the time of its first release. It certainly surpassed predicted sales for a debut feature by a relatively unknown *Cahiers du cinéma* director, even following Truffaut's success at Cannes in the spring of 1959. Almost 260,000 people saw the film in the seven weeks of its first run in Paris, which already represented more than half the tickets sold all over France by Truffaut's *Les Quatre cents coups*. The eventual profit (rumoured to be fifty times the investment) was further increased through sales for international distribution following the 1960 Cannes Film Festival, despite the last-minute exclusion of the film from the list of features nominated to represent France in the official competition, as the minister of culture, André Malraux, preferred to include *Moderato cantabile*, Peter Brook's adaptation of the novel by Marguerite Duras which also starred Jean-Paul Belmondo.[1]

But what now seems even more extraordinary for a film that could have easily been categorised as an art-house, independent production is that it managed to combine commercial success with critical acclaim. Godard made the most of the unconventional working methods associated with the New Wave not just to keep costs to a minimum, but also to promote a radically different notion of cinema and – last but not least – to publicise his own image as the iconoclastic *auteur* deliberately breaking the mould. If his compulsive cross-references to Hollywood classics and his in-jokes managed to annoy some of his natural allies, absolutely no one (either inside or outside the *Cahiers du cinéma* circle) could fail to notice that with *À bout de souffle* Godard effectively delivered the manifesto of the new generation, the distinctive template for a cinema emerging out of the New Wave ideas. Asked to describe the *Nouvelle vague* 'style' in 1963, Jean-Pierre Melville, the director who made a cameo appearance in *À bout de souffle* as Parvulesco, declared: 'The "new wave" style does not exist: but if it did, it would purely and simply be the style of Godard.'[2] Truffaut himself did not hesitate to argue that *À bout de souffle* 'marked a decisive turn in the history of cinema, like *Citizen Kane* in 1940'.[3] This resonates with Godard's declared intention when he embarked upon his debut feature. It is obvious from the recurrent formal cross-references in *À bout de souffle*, as well as from Godard's statements to the press, that Orson Welles's youthful masterpiece was the kind of cinematic landmark that the New Wave director set out to match. But why was Godard's debut feature so successful in promoting and illustrating the *Cahiers* ideology? What exactly persuaded the critics and the public that this film rather than any other captured the aesthetic programme of the new generation? The answer is twofold, as it reflects, on the one hand, Godard's provocative rewriting of a genre film to pass self-reflective comment on the evolution of cinema and, on the other, his skilful handling of the publicity campaign that preceded the release of *À bout de souffle*. As Colin MacCabe rightly observed, 'never can a film that cost so little have had such a huge launch'.[4]

## Film Launch and First Reception

After only four weeks of shooting (from 17 August to 15 September 1959), *À bout de souffle* went into post-production. Another two months passed before the sneak previews, but Godard and Richard Balducci, the press attaché, who had already arranged the extensive coverage of the shoot, started a concerted promotional operation on several fronts that turned out to be extremely efficient. In October 1959, a young journalist with *France-Observateur*, Marc Pierret (whom Balducci had planted in the crew), published his daily observations on every atypical aspect of the production likely to stir the curiosity of the specialists and increase box office numbers. Presented as 'the log book of an apprentice *cinéaste*', the article conveyed the impromptu quality of the film's dialogue, and made some tantalising revelations about last minute casting decisions or the cameraman's previous experience as a war photographer, without neverthe-less giving away the plot or indeed anticipating the yet undecided ending, as Godard was allegedly still considering whether or not to kill his protagonist.[5] Apart from the on-set report, unusual for a small budget debut feature, the still photographer present at the shoot, Raymond Cauchetier, provided some of the more spectacular illustrations for the press reviews, such as the image of Godard pushing the post-office mail cart from which Raoul Coutard was filming the Champs-Élysées sequence. Cauchetier had already worked with the producer, Georges de Beauregard, in 1958, on *Pêcheur d'Islande* for which Godard wrote the dialogues. The press attaché himself, Richard Balducci, who made a cameo appearance in the film as Tolmatchoff, alongside several of Godard's friends from the *Cahiers* group (Jean Domarchi – the mugged man in the toilets; Jean Douchet – the driver of the 4CV; Jacques Siclier and

André S. Labarthe – journalists interviewing Parvulesco at Orly), belonged to a tightly knit community of young critics and film professionals who variously contributed to an astounding publicity scoop, all the while promoting their own venture. In advance of the public release, Balducci compiled a very effective press portfolio, including an array of statements from celebrities whom he invited to the sneak preview: Jean-Paul Sartre, Francis Jeanson, Jean Cocteau, Françoise Sagan, Joseph Kessel, Jacques Becker, Sophia Loren and Carlo Ponti. Some commentators, such as René Guyonnet in *L'Express* and Georges Charensol in *Les Nouvelles littéraires*, chose to relay the first enthusiastic celebrity quips instead of any opening statement: "'It's really very beautiful" said Jean-Paul Sartre, "It's fantastic" declared Sophia Loren';[6] "'A real gem [*une merveille*]" cried out Jean Cocteau, "I've never seen anything like it!" exclaimed Henri Jeanson.[7] Moreover, in the crucial months before the public release, contradictory rumours started circulating about the film: 'It's the worst film of the year', 'It cannot be edited, there are only jump cuts in it' or, conversely: 'It's a magnificent film', 'the New Wave masterpiece, the *Citizen Kane* of the young French cinema'.[8] The debates were cleverly orchestrated by Godard and Richard Balducci. Making full use of his short-lived but instructive experience as press attaché at Fox (where he replaced Chabrol in 1958), Godard combined the more common gathering of testimonials from celebrities with a new strategy for disseminating his ideas and building his reputation: interviews. His biographer, Richard Brody, aptly summed up the filmmaker's unprecedented use of the reporting media:

> As the director of a film born of a unique mode of production and philosophical orientation, he also required the appropriate conditions for a correct appreciation of his unusual work. He needed, in other words, to generate – and to induce critics to employ – a method of criticism that was apt for his own film. This was his self-appointed task as an interviewee.[9]

The need to guide the less discerning critic and viewer actually corresponded to the self-referential character of the work itself and can be said to highlight Godard's attitude as one of the first, if not *the* first, postmodern *auteur*, consciously blending the fictional and critical layers of discourse in order to expose and break down cinematic conventions. Whereas in his first interview, published in *France-Observateur*, Godard seemed content to puzzle his readers with a string of paradoxical remarks about cinema,[10] in *Le Monde* he set out to explain his view of the characters and the relevance of the diegetic music for the film's doomed love story:

> Things can't work out between them because he thinks about death and she doesn't. [...] For a long time the boy has been obsessed by death, he has forebodings. That's the reason why I shot that scene of the accident where he sees a guy die in the street. I quoted that sentence from Lenin, 'We are all dead people on leave', and I chose the *Clarinet Concerto* that Mozart wrote shortly before dying.[11]

Not everyone rejoiced in the knowledge of this unsuspected depth and complexity of interaction between image and sound applied to a mock Hollywood thriller. The Catholic critics, Godard's least enthusiastic commentators (with the sole exception of the left-wing magazine, *Positif*), argued that the link between the scene in which Poiccard has an early premonition of his tragic end and the moment when, just before the denouement, the *Clarinet Concerto* is heard on the soundtrack is at best strenuous and requires specialist knowledge of music and 'an acute sense of symbols'[12] – at least as far as their role in Godard's filmic syntax was concerned. Jean Rochereau, writing for the newspaper *La Croix*, found that the theme of the film was 'sordid and *cliché*', the dialogues were 'arbitrary and conventional, full of trivial puns, of unprintable rude words, and totally improbable scenes'.[13] The *Premier Plan* critic, Raymond Borde, likened Poiccard to 'a paratrooper on leave', and denounced his 'profound adherence to the values of law and order'.[14]

Yet Godard was perfectly aware that he was redefining narrative codes and bringing forth a new cinematic language, based on an unprecedented critical re-appropriation of the entire history of cinema and its gamut of expressive techniques. For the New Wave *auteur* was first and foremost a *cinéphile*, and all the debut features of the young directors, as Godard often recalled, were the work of film enthusiasts: 'we were the first directors to know that Griffith exists';[15] 'we knew that we came after Eisenstein, after Rossellini'.[16] The impressive number of visual citations or references to Hollywood classics, to Italian Neo-Realism or Russian montage did not elude those who were already familiar with the *Cahiers* ideology, and on both sides of the Channel critics hailed the birth of an indubitable *auteur*. 'This film carries the mark of an auteur. And this auteur is Jean-Luc Godard' – concluded Jean de Baroncelli in *Le Monde*, after having praised the offhand manner in which Godard 'uses cinematographic language'.[17] 'The cinema is not a trade. It isn't team-work' – declared Louis Marcorelles in *Sight and Sound* – 'One is always alone while shooting, as though facing a blank page [...]. Instead of writing a novel, Godard *writes* a film ...'[18] And, more explicitly, Gérald Devries stated: 'Despite the homage paid to a certain American cinema, and in particular to Humphrey Bogart, Jean-Luc Godard shows total indifference to traditional technique. In fact, here is the first work genuinely written with a camera-pen.'[19]

But the ground for such defining statements had been prepared, among other things, by Truffaut's interview published before the sneak preview, on 4 October 1959 in *Radio-Cinéma-Télévision*: 'Godard films the way he writes. He made each of his short films in 24 hours. He possesses an extraordinary ease. And as holding the camera in one's hand is a rather tiring exercise, the cameraman himself wants to work fast. The result is surprisingly graceful and elegant.'[20] Speaking from the position of an award winner at Cannes, Truffaut commended the film for which he was supposed to have written the scenario by nevertheless giving Godard full credit for the ingenuity of the treatment and of the shooting style: 'The pretext is unimportant. What counts – and what is stunning – is what Godard has done with it'; and he follows this up with one of the earliest specific descriptions of the New Wave style (under the heading: 'A Revolutionary Technique: The Hand-held Camera'):

> There has been a lot of talk about the New Wave methods and yet no one has so far been able to define their revolutionary character. With À bout de souffle, one can speak of a technique which is unusual, to say the least. This film was shot in four weeks (a normal film requires at least eight). Only three professional actors [featured]: Jean-Paul Belmondo, Jean Seberg and Claude Mansard. All the other parts were played by members of the crew or of the production team, including the producers and the press attaché. No dialogue was written down. They were all improvised on the spot. Everything was shot outdoors or in real indoor locations. Finally, and above all, the camera was always hand-held. [...] The novelty is not the amateur technique [itself] but the fact that it is *deliberately* used by a filmmaker who otherwise has every means to shoot in the most comfortable manner.[21]

However arguable some of Truffaut's remarks may seem in retrospect (such as the implied disconnection between financial constraints and technical innovation), the legend of À bout de souffle was born long before the public release and, to a certain extent (if we are to judge from Balducci's press portfolio and Godard and Truffaut's interviews), even before the successful previews in Paris, Lyon and Marseille. In December 1959 Michèle Manceaux's interview with Godard in L'Express made sensational revelations about the young cinéaste's brushes with the law as a petty criminal strangely akin to the protagonist of À bout de souffle: 'He broke into a safe, got himself locked in an insane asylum, and even took off with the cash box at Cahiers'.[22] But Godard's self-styled image as the enfant terrible of the French cinema seemed to take its cue not so much from Truffaut's by then famous Les quatre cents coups than from the possible association with Nicholas Ray's 1955 feature Rebel Without A Cause: 'I broke into the safe because I was waiting for a girl who didn't show up and I really had to do something. Rebellion without a cause, as they say in America'.[23] Was, then, Belmondo's screen persona destined to become the icon of disenchanted youth like James Dean? In any case Godard made sure that *his* measuring up against Hollywood directors did not go unnoticed. And his freshly established reputation as the spearhead of New Wave rebellion gathered momentum with declarations such as Gilbert Salachas's praising of the 'spectacular anarchy in tone, the images, the language' whose 'extremism in its originality is presented almost as a manifesto'.[24] In his turn, the film historian and critic Jacques Siclier described À bout de souffle in unambiguous terms as 'the manifesto of the Nouvelle Vague' and stated that: 'In the light of Breathless, The 400 Blows looks like an obedient schoolboy's homework, Chabrol's films the product of a perfect academicism'.[25] Similarly, Georges Sadoul, who labelled Godard's first feature the Quai des brumes of 1960 (in a paradoxical reference back to Carné's masterpiece of Poetic Realism) argued that: 'As far as sheer competence is concerned, Godard could teach Truffaut and Chabrol a thing or two: their first films were clumsy efforts compared with À bout de souffle'.[26]

Among the less flattering comments, Sadoul queried the ostentatious amorality of the two protagonists, the sloppy style of the photography and editing that could easily become 'the *clichés* of tomorrow', while judging the leftist credentials of Godard's 'anarchism' unconvincing. Raymond Borde equally found Belmondo's reputation as an anarchist 'laughable' and put Godard's stylistic innovations down to 'sheer amateurism'.[27] The ambiguous moral and political stance portrayed in the film prompted occasionally scathing remarks from the left as well as the right-wing journalists. René Cortade denounced 'the type of anarcho-fascist ideal that is unleashed by the film',[28] while Louis Seguin, in the left-wing *Positif* (the rival of *Cahiers du cinéma*), likened Poiccard to 'one of those guys who writes "Death to Jews" on the walls of the metro and spells it wrong'.[29] As part of a concerted attack on the *Nouvelle Vague*, Freddy Buache declared that: '*Breathless* poses the first unambiguous prototype of the Fascist arrogance that is hiding in the trough of the New Wave'.[30] Throughout his early career Godard struggled to prove his commitment to left-wing ideals although his overtly political fiction films (*Le Petit Soldat* [1960] and *Les Carabiniers* [1963]) continued to arouse fierce controversy and failed to satisfy either side of the political spectrum.

In retrospect, *À bout de souffle* marked a turning point in the history of the *Nouvelle Vague* and was an instant success on its general release on 16 March 1960. René Pignères's SNC-Impéria gave the film the classic opening for 'big films' in four of the best cinemas in Paris: Balzac, Helder, Scala and Vivienne. Columbia released the soundtrack record with Martial Solal's music, the Seghers publishing house brought out Claude Francolin's novel inspired by the story of the film in February 1960 and in the same month the film won the prestigious Jean Vigo award. Luc Moullet's landmark review, published in *Cahiers du cinéma*, highlighted Godard's 'ability to make films not just aimed at art-house audiences, but capable of having successful runs in such legendary Paris cinemas as the Gaumont-Palace, the Midi-Minuit, the Normandie, the Balzac, the Helder, the Scala, the Vivienne or the Radio-Cité'.[31] Moullet was not the only critic to remark on the 'ethnological' quality of Godard's portrayal of disaffected youth. Pierre Macabru, in *Combat*, had already drawn a parallel between Godard's use of improvised dialogue and Jean Rouch's much-celebrated documentaries such as *Moi, un noir* that won the Prix Louis Delluc in 1957.

Following its successful showing out of competition at Cannes, *À bout de souffle* was sold for distribution to countries around the world and opened to mainly positive reviews in New York in February 1961 and in England in July 1961. Brosley Crowther's review in *The New York Times* highlighted the stylistic audacity of the film: '[*Breathless*] goes at its unattractive subject in an eccentric photographic style that sharply conveys the nervous tempo and the emotional erraticalness [sic] of the story it tells'.[32] Arlene Croce in *Film Quarterly* described Godard's debut as 'cinematic jazz',[33] while Dwight MacDonald argued that 'the sound film, after thirty years of fumbling around, [was] beginning to develop a style of its own' as seen in *Breathless*, (Antonioni's) *L'Avventura* or (Resnais's)

*Hiroshima mon amour*, all of which 'restored montage and the camera to the dominance they had before they were dethroned by stage dialogue in 1930'.[34]

By the time *À bout de souffle* reached London, the multimedia publicity campaign that accompanied the French release had already established the film's emblematic status and *The Times* could confidently state: '*Breathless* is in the fashionable idiom, a *nouvelle vague* film, a production of the *Cahiers du cinéma* group [...] It is the group's "intellectual manifesto".'[35]

### *Breathless*: The American Remake

The warm reception of *Breathless* in the USA came at a time when the ideology of the *Cahiers* group was already beginning to make an impact on the young generation of American film critics and directors. The French re-appraisal of mainstream studio directors (such as Hitchcock, Hawks, Nicholas Ray, Douglas Sirk and Anthony Mann), coupled with the 'first-person' cinema that Truffaut had pioneered, taught the aspiring American directors that filmmaking had more to do with low-budget experimentation and telling stories of one's own experience than with old-time 'production values'.

Given the popularity and commercial success of *À bout de souffle* it is not surprising that Godard himself initially envisaged the possibility of shooting a remake in 1975. He approached his producer, Georges de Beauregard, with the idea of using 'the same budget as in 1959' and submitted a project entitled *À bout de souffle numéro deux* to the CNC. There was little, apart from the budget and the first part of the title (which was eventually dropped), that remained of the original film. Coming after Godard's collaboration with Jean-Pierre Gorin in the Dziga Vertov group, born out of the political militancy of May 1968, *Numéro deux* [Number Two, 1975] provided a grim meditation on the alienation of individuals through work and the violence of sexual relationships in a married couple. Although this was the first fiction feature co-authored with Anne-Marie Miéville, his partner from the mid-1970s onwards, *Numéro deux* is still redolent of the doctrinaire concerns that defined the Dziga Vertov productions.

Around the same time an American underground director, Jim McBride, was looking for a scenario or a book that would prove attractive for a Hollywood producer likely to invest in new talent. However, compared to the time when the New Wave *cinéastes* had their first break in Europe, opportunities in the mid- to late 1970s Hollywood were few and far between. Across the Atlantic, the film industry had remained highly conservative despite the resounding success of the French *politique des auteurs* with part of the specialised press and the young underground practitioners. The situation, as Jim McBride described it, resembled a return to the tried and tested methods of the old studio system in place at the time when Godard and Truffaut were preparing their own revolution against the *cinéma de papa*: 'I'd been here [in Los Angeles] for a couple of years, getting nowhere. People would tell me I was an unknown quantity and had to associate myself with something like a book or a play that had its own currency if I was going to succeed.'[36] Hence the idea of a remake, and in particular the idea of remaking *Breathless* which, according to McBride's recollection, 'had a mystique attached to it, even among people who had never seen it'.[37] Godard's first feature had made a lasting impression on Jim McBride and the co-writer of the remake script, L.M. Kit Carson, also remembered being 'devastated' by the showing of *À bout de souffle* in 1961, which he attended after reading Brosley Crowther's review in *The New York Times*. Both McBride and Carson were persuaded of the merits of returning this maverick French *film noir* to its American roots, and by 1978 the producer Martin Erlichman had secured a deal with Universal. Gary Busey was supposed to play the male lead, but the deal with Universal fell through and Jim McBride struggled to get several other prominent actors interested in the part (including Robert De Niro, John Travolta and Al Pacino) before Richard Gere eventually agreed, 'provided that he could play a more active part in the production than he had played in any of his previous films'.[38] The star of *American Gigolo* (1980) ended up playing a part in rewriting the script as well as in casting and hiring the crew. The script went through no fewer than seven revisions which, although not surprising for a remake, signalled a clear departure from Godard's improvised dialogue and emphasis on *mise-en-scène* and editing. But a considerably greater constraint in McBride's case which determined all other aspects of production, including the script, was working within the Hollywood film industry. Leaving behind a fairly successful, if short, career as an independent filmmaker and embarking on one's first Hollywood directorial project, with a $1.5 million budget, is something that comes with strings attached, as McBride himself admitted:

> Godard's movie was made for no money, on the streets of Paris, with a bunch of friends. And it grew out of the French intellectual milieu that I was partial to. Our version is much more expensive and much less cerebral. It's more passionate and emotional, though the emotions are exaggerated in the way that Hollywood movies used to be.[39]

Whereas Godard's feature self-consciously displays its mock *film noir* credentials, the closest established genre that McBride's remake seems to emulate is the popular melodrama. Not only does Michel Poiccard become quite a likeable character, devoid of misogynistic and cynical traits, but his emotions are emphatically stated and the morally unacceptable edges are smoothed out to allow the audience to sympathise with his plight. Poiccard's insulting direct camera address during the road sequence ('If you don't like the sea …') is replaced by the innocuous: 'Just look at the sky!' – a pointless reminder of cinematographer Richard Kline's picture-postcard sunset over the Mojave desert. But, in the same manner in which the Marseille–Paris journey turned into a Las Vegas–Los Angeles ride (symbolically getting ever closer to Hollywood's home base), Godard's tribute to black-and-white 1950s thrillers and his experimental use of highly sensitive film stock curiously translated into a celebration of hyper-realistic Technicolor.

The Hollywood version preserved the idea of a Franco-American 'encounter' but swapped the nationality of the protagonists: an American small-time car thief named Jesse Lujack (Richard Gere) falls in love with a French architecture student, Monica Poiccard (Valérie Kaprisky). However, apart from ensuring that the 'cerebral' pursuits remain confined to the French side, which in turn make Jesse, a comic-book and rock-and-roll fan, look decidedly simple-minded at times, McBride's film has no intention of staging a confrontation between Hollywood and the New Wave. The remake seems to take Godard's dedication to Monogram Pictures quite literally and proceeds to return the narrative and the *mise-en-scène* to their American sources with undiscerning faithfulness. According to the French film critic Serge Daney's apt remark:

> *Breathless – made in USA* does not betray Godard (it would have been formidable and anyway Godardian). It doesn't re-interpret him, it plays as if nothing has happened or rather as if, after all, a Franco-Swiss director had by mistake made an American B-movie in 1960 in Paris.[40]

And Vincent Canby's review in *The New York Times* interestingly seemed to agree on this point: 'Mr. McBride's *Breathless*, though it keeps amazingly close to the original in its details, is more like a high-class *Dirty Mary Crazy Harry*, John Hough's 1974 B-picture that gained a large and dedicated following among the serious and not so serious.'[41] Other European and American reviewers were more forgiving but, nonetheless, for the 'French film fans', in the words of Jeremy Richey, *Breathless* 'was the equivalent of remaking *Citizen Kane*'.[42] And the end result was not so much 'a colourful American tribute to the French New Wave'[43] as a homage to the Hollywood entertainment industry whose codes and practices Godard aimed to dismantle.

Admittedly, the possibility of a parodic, second-degree reading of Jesse Lujack's story is briefly suggested in the opening shots in which the protagonist, in gaudy 1970s attire (an obvious parody of Gere's earlier screen persona in *American Gigolo*), can be seen reading the comic book adventures of his role model, the Silver Surfer. But the self-reflexive and intertextual connotations stop here, as there is virtually nothing left of the provocative cinematography, in-jokes and montage of Godard's film. Jim McBride's *Breathless* is too one-sided in its reappraisal of the Hollywood blueprint to pay any attention to what made *À bout de souffle* such an inspired French parody of genre conventions, a Trojan-horse attack on the bastion of continuity editing. But then the American director already started off on the wrong foot by believing that the story in itself was strong enough to stand the translation:

> The story has a classic opposition of characters. It's about a man who acts without thinking and a girl who thinks too much. I identified with that conflict when I first saw the movie, and I don't think that has been lost in our version. One of the things that was so powerful about the original was that it was about two people who were constantly misconnecting. I think that's what made *Breathless* more accessible than

any of Godard's other movies. It said a lot of truthful things about the relations between men and women that films don't usually say.[44]

Everyone who has seen Godard's first feature knows that its striking ingenuity does not reside in the rather conventional plot but in the visual style and underlying polemic with Hollywood classics. Falling well short of being a mixed-media experiment (such as Robert Zemeckis's *Who Framed Roger Rabbit* [1988]), Jim McBride's *Breathless* uses Jesse's identification with the Silver Surfer alongside rather than in opposition to conventional film narrative and editing. Images of the comic strip adventures are intercut with images of Jesse at various points during the film, but these occurrences only serve to underline a pervading concern with the hyper-realism of saturated colours (such as the spectacular sunset in the road sequence) and the corresponding pop-art aesthetics of the Los Angeles' murals, which McBride explores at great length in the second half of his film. The emphasis on *décor* and carefully orchestrated, beautiful shots *per se* ended up exasperating even some of the American viewers and critics:

> If anything, *Breathless* looks too good for its own good. Richard Sylbert's production design is still another example of high cinema chic. There can't be a single Los Angeles wall mural that doesn't turn up as a background at one point or another, so frequently, in fact, that there are times one wishes the camera would let us look at the art work and forget the actors.[45]

It is obvious that whereas Godard saw his experimental first feature as a documentary on the two main actors, McBride preferred to highlight the pop-art visual attractions of the city and its architecture (Monica Poiccard's chosen profession). And the inconspicuous link between middle-class Monica and the small-time thief Jesse Lujack, was provided by Jesse's other idol, the rock-and-roll legend, Jerry Lee Lewis. On his way from Las Vegas to Los Angeles, Jesse finds and plays a cassette with Jerry Lee Lewis's hit *Breathless*, which first made it to number one in the charts in 1958, and which becomes the leitmotif of the eponymous movie. In the same manner in which the comic-book hyper-aesthetics and the Andy Warhol-type depictions of emotion dominate the *mise-en-scène* and acting, the sound of Jerry Lee Lewis defines the film score. As one of the more enthusiastic reviewers remarked:

> McBride's *Breathless* plays like a compulsive and flashy pop art piece; one that you stare at for awhile [sic] trying to figure out whether or not it is actually art or just something hanging on the wall. With its whirlwind pace, Jack Nitzsche score and stunning splashes of sun stroked Los Angeles color, *Breathless* is undeniably fun and exciting.[46]

It could be argued that the recurrent alternation of comic strip images with images of Jesse echoed Godard's similar use of advertising and comic strips in *Pierrot le fou* (1965), a worthy sequel to *À bout de souffle* featuring Belmondo and illustrating the same parodic, subversive filmmaking style which set the

*Nouvelle Vague* director apart, yet almost entirely eluded Jim McBride's approach to the remake. However *Breathless* had a very successful first run and made just short of $20 million on the American market alone. A novel based on the film by Leonore Fleischer was published in 1983 and translated into French as *À bout de souffle – Made in USA*. Jim McBride's remake opened to mixed reviews in Paris, where some critics rightly contrasted Michel Poiccard's existential obsession with death (underscored by Martial Solal's inspired jazz music) and Jesse Lujack's 'permanent exaltation', his passion for Jerry Lee Lewis and his admiration for the comic-book hero's 'infantile idealism'.[47] Jim McBride went on to make a biopic of the rock-and-roll legend in 1989, entitled *Great Balls of Fire*. *Breathless* was released on DVD in the USA, Canada and US territories in 2000. It was released again by MGM Home Entertainment in March 2001 for region 2, and in a double pack with *Red Corner* (another B-type thriller featuring Richard Gere in the lead role) in 2003.

### Cinema after Godard: The Critical and Cinematic Legacy

*À bout de souffle* had a considerable impact on the French and the American cultural scene during the early 1960s and its influence has never ceased to grow. Over the years, its reputation as the New Wave manifesto that inaugurated the postmodern rewriting of genre and editing codes turned a small-budget mock thriller into an all-time cult classic. The early screenings of *À bout de souffle* in the US determined the career of young critics and aspiring directors. Godard's extensive knowledge of cinema and provocative dismantling of conventions inspired a range of like-minded independent filmmakers, such as Martin Scorsese, Francis Coppola, John Cassavetes and Quentin Tarantino, who went on to become respected *auteurs* in their own terms and transformed the audience's perception of Hollywood genre films. Even McBride's remake benefited from the rage surrounding the original. Tarantino famously declared his preference for the remake,[48] although his entire career, since *Reservoir Dogs* (1992) and *Pulp Fiction* (1994) in particular, obviously displays his stylistic and conceptual indebtedness to Godard. His production company, A Band Apart, named after Godard's 1964 feature *Bande à part*, paid homage to the New Wave director's idiosyncratic use of stereotypical characters and highly-formalised second-rate plots (e.g. the B-series thriller) to pass self-reflexive comment on the means and limitations of cinema. Similarly, discerning film buffs were surprised to see that Luc Besson, one of the representatives of the French *Cinéma du Look*, the New New Wave of the 1980s, actually based a car theft scene in *Subway* (1985) on Jim McBride's remake rather than on Godard's original. For the observers on the other side of the Atlantic, this indirect quotation signalled 'Besson's sly wink to a sadly underrated and mostly forgotten American film'.[49]

The displayed awareness of the cinematic history that has preceded a new director's appearance on the scene was one of the key lessons to be learned from

Godard's debut feature. It was not simply a question of mastering the shooting technique and the established narrative codes. Otherwise, who could deny that McBride's classical chase scenes and use of background *décors* turned out to be infinitely better handled than Godard's 'fumbled' editing and lagging pace of action (only mended by jump cuts at post-production stage)? What the New Wave radical departure from conventions taught some if not all the young American directors coming of age in the 1960s and 1970s was that the critical discourse and the use of filmic citation and cross-referencing, parody and pastiche can and should become part of the individual style if new ways of making and viewing films were to replace the old. In any case, cinema could never be the same after *À bout de souffle*, as film critics and practitioners on both sides of the Atlantic recognised: 'A radical break with all current technical conventions, an obvious taste for provocation led Jean-Luc Godard to re-invent cinema', declared Jacques Siclier,[50] and thirty years later the American film critic and historian Wheeler Winston Dixon concluded: 'an opportunity came knocking that would permanently alter the course of Jean-Luc Godard's life, and change the face of cinema forever, not only in France and the United States, but throughout the entire cinema community'.[51]

Godard's subsequent career, which radicalised his polemical stand against Hollywood's commercial methods and standardised film narrative, convinced observers of his lasting influence on independent art circuits in the US and further afield, so that by 1980 Annette Insdorf in *The New York Times* could rightly conclude that:

> Whether it was his jump cuts, fragmented narratives or his exhibition of play-ful awareness of filmmaking history through references to other films and early techniques, he engaged the viewer in a new relationship to the screen, namely an intellectual challenge.[52]

In fact, the 1980s marked not only the release of Jim McBride's controversial remake, but also the broadcast of *À bout de souffle* on French television in 1985, followed by the French and British second theatrical release of Godard's feature in 1988. Jacques Richard's review of the premiere on the French TV channel TF1 highlighted the long-term impact of Godard's film: 'This "vandal" of the cinematographic narrative did more than destroy. Nothing has ever been the same since the electroshock that he inflicted on the seventh art in the 1960s: not all doors that cinema saw opening before it looked onto an abyss'.[53] In *Le Quotidien*, George-Marc Benamou described *À bout de souffle* as 'the film of a generation that has not aged. It may be dated, but it is not yet out of date'.[54] British commentators greeted the second theatrical release, in 1988, with the same enthusiasm as their French counterparts. According to George Perry in *The Sunday Times*: 'Often the pace-setting films are the ones in which the *clichés* are invented. Looking at them anew years later can prove disappointing, the freshness having been squeezed out by subsequent imitations. A pleasure, then, to report that Jean-Luc Godard's *À bout de souffle* [...] is as exciting as ever'.[55]

Five years earlier, disappointed with McBride's film, Alexandre Astruc preferred to cast a nostalgic glance back at the New Wave's love at first sight (*coup de foudre*) and the youthful rebellion against conventionalism that accompanied Godard's debut:

> More than *The 400 Blows* or *Le Beau Serge*, *À bout de souffle* marked our generation and this remake can only make us feel nostalgic. […] The great merit of *À bout de souffle* is that it opened the doors, it shattered the conformist cinema that hung over us like a leaden weight. The lesson in all this is that one must not play around with a masterpiece, and try to rekindle the flame that is still burning in our hearts. Better let our memory rest in peace. There is no point in trying to resuscitate it with a mediocre film.[56]

At about the same time, the new French generation of directors who made their debut in the early 1980s and became known under the banner of the *Cinéma du Look* (grouping mainly Jean-Jacques Beineix, Luc Besson and Leos Carax) started to acquire the reputation of legitimate heirs of Godard's revolution. Not only were they privileging the kind of hyper-aesthetics and pop-art or comic strip *décor* which prompted parallels with Godard's use of cartoon images and advertising billboards in *Pierrot le fou* or *Weekend*, but they also showed a technical prowess and ingenious pastiche of disparate codes and genres that echoed Godard's own defiant break with narrative conventions. The new trend came to the attention of the critics and the general public when the video-clip montage, the use of 'flat' colours and pop-art *décors* in Beineix's *Diva* (1982) were rewarded with a flurry of César awards followed by enthusiastic reviews on both sides of the Channel. Martyn Auty in *Sight and Sound* commented on Godard's legacy in this stylish 'post-punk' adaptation of a thriller by Delacorta:

> In his use of classical music in modernist settings Beineix has been compared to the young Godard. The most apposite cross-reference would be to *À bout de souffle*. Both films display their affection for Hollywood cinema and Americana through a gangster movie plot and the relationship between a Frenchman and an American woman, and both represent a distinctive departure from the ossifying conventions of the national cinema from which they spring.[57]

The advent of the *Cinéma du Look* coincided with the rediscovery of the American and the French thriller novels, whose adaptations for the screen often yielded improbable, hastily assembled plots used as a pretext for flamboyant visual effects and stunning *décors*. Beineix's postmodern take on the classic *film noir* genre deliberately mixed distinct narrative codes and clashing cultural registers in the *mise-en-scène* as well as on the soundtrack. The careful blending of diegetic and non-diegetic music, coupled with a decisive shift in the directorial focus on sound rather than just visual montage, set the new generation apart. This aspect could have elicited further comparisons with Godard's use of jazz, classical music or background noise as part of a strategy fostering the audience's active critical involvement as opposed to the passive consumerist viewing, if it wasn't for the total disinterest in politics that critics detected in all the productions associated with the *Cinéma du Look*. Similar accusations of right-wing allegiances or political apathy to those that had plagued *À bout de souffle* at its first release were levelled at Beineix's *Diva*, Carax's *Les Amants du Pont-Neuf* (1991) and Besson's *Nikita* (1990), which seemed impervious to contemporary debates on racial, sexual and social inequalities, while emulating the Hollywood entertainment pattern even though in the pastiche, self-reflexive mode inaugurated by Godard. Out of the three young directors, Carax seems to have attracted the most consistent parallels with Godard, partly because of his fascination with the legendary Godard–Anna Karina couple, and partly because of the entangled relationship that filmmaking for him entertains with seduction and miscommunication: 'that's how it started – it was always a machine and a girl'[58] (a close paraphrase of Godard's famous: 'All you need to make a movie is a girl and a gun'). As David Thompson remarked at the UK release of *Les Amants du Pont-Neuf* in 1992:

> His first film, *Boy Meets Girl* (1983), was a black-and-white trip through a Paris night haunted by the spectre of Godard: a fragmented dream of post-adolescent yearnings and an encyclopaedia for alienation freaks. [...] With its futuristic thriller setting, *Mauvais Sang* (1986) may tip its hat to Godard's *Alphaville*, but the stunningly composed colour photography of Jean-Yves Escoffier and the intensely musical performances of the cast [...] announced that a distinctive Carax style had arrived.[59]

The French film historians and critics equally placed *Mauvais Sang* under the 'joint auspices of *À bout de souffle* and *Alphaville*',[60] while Carax himself admitted seeing 'a lot of Godard' during his formative years, when Serge Daney, general editor of *Cahiers du cinéma* during the 1970s, played the role that André Bazin had played for the New Wave directors a couple of decades earlier.

In 1993, the release of *À bout de souffle* on VHS, enjoyed a warm reception in the UK and the USA. According to Mark Kermode's comments on the inside cover of the UK video version:

> Watching *À bout de souffle* again, against the frequently dreary background of formulaic nineties' cinema the prime response which the film elicits is not intellectual or critical, but visceral; a simple joy at the sheer bloody-minded vitality of the piece. [...] Many celluloid 'milestones' overturn cinematic conventions simply to become unwatchable time-pieces, but *À bout de souffle* seems perversely to have improved with age. [...] The film has lost none of its surging power.[61]

Godard's legendary debut feature was released on DVD in 2000 (region 2) and 2001 (all regions). Martial Solal's music for the film was remastered and released on CD by Sonic Music and Universal Music in 2002, accompanied by an interview with the composer who had rendered the jazz score of *À bout de souffle* as famous as Godard's freestyle montage: 'There's a correspondence between *À bout de souffle* and jazz: a freedom of expression that also passes into the chorus from the soloists, Pierre Gossez on saxophone and Roger Guérin on trumpet. Godard deliberately destroys any form of classical construction.'[62] The famous correlation between the musical score and the revolutionary visual style of Godard's debut feature has contributed to the cult status that *À bout de souffle* has enjoyed for half a century. Yet the extraordinary longevity of this self-conscious tale about the means and the ends of filmic language can no less be attributed to its carefully orchestrated critical reception at the time of its first release, than to the manner in which successive generations of young directors (from Quentin Tarantino to Jean-Jacques Beineix and Léos Carax) have paid tribute to its groundbreaking impact on the history of cinema, and thus re-acquainted audiences, at regular intervals, with an enduring legacy of iconoclastic filmmaking.

## Notes

1    See Richard Brody, *Everything is Cinema: The Working Life of Jean-Luc Godard*, London: Faber and Faber, 2008, p. 99.

2    Jean-Pierre Melville in *L'Avant-scène cinéma*, No. 24, 15 March 1963 (quoted in Francis Courtade, *Les Malédictions du cinéma français. Une histoire du cinéma français parlant 1928–1978*, Paris: Éditions Alain Moreau, 1978 p. 279).

3    François Truffaut cited by Jean Wagner, 'À bout de souffle ou le monde en porte à faux', in À bout de souffle, *dialogue et continuité photographique*, Paris: Balland, 1974 (see Michel Marie, *Comprendre Godard. Travelling avant sur* À bout de souffle *et* Le Mépris, Paris: Armand Collin, 2006, pp. 142–143.

4    Colin MacCabe, *Godard. A Portrait of the Artist at 70*, London: Bloomsbury, 2003, p. 122.

5    Marc Pierret, 'Carnet de bord d'un apprenti cinéaste', *France-Observateur*, 29 October 1959, p. 1. The famous French novelist L.-F. Céline was supposed to play Parvulesco's part in the film. Raoul Coutard's reputation as an experienced photographer and war correspondent in Vietnam was also thrown in for good measure. Nevertheless, this implicit association with right-wing politics fuelled some of the most savage attacks against À bout de souffle (such as Louis Seguin's review in *Positif*, April 1960), and the same accusations came back to haunt Godard after the mixed reception of *Le Petit Soldat*.

6    G. Charensol, 'À bout de souffle du côté de Hollywood...', *Les Nouvelles littéraires*, 24 March 1960.

7    René Guyonnet, 'À bout de souffle', *L'Express*, 17 March 1960.

8    See Marie, *À bout de souffle*, op. cit., p. 115.

9    Richard Brody, op. cit., p. 74.

10   Asked whether he likes the cinema, Godard replies: 'I despise it. It is nothing. It does not exist. This is why it is beautiful. Therefore I like it', in Pierret, op. cit.

11   *Le Monde*, 18 March 1960.

12   André Bessèges, *France Catholique*, 25 March 1960.

13   Jean Rochereau, *La Croix*, 30 March 1960.

14   Raymond Borde, 'Cinéma français d'aujourd'hui', in Raymond Borde, Freddy Buache and Jean Curtelin, *Nouvelle Vague*, Lyon: Premier Plan/Serdoc, 1962, p. 21.

15   Godard in Milne, 1999, p. 172.

16   Godard, 'Cultivons notre jardin', interview for the magazine *VO Réalités*, July 1989, reproduced in *Gen Lock*, No. 15, December 1989, p. 14.

17   Jean de Baroncelli, 'Le premier grand film de Jean-Luc Godard, *À bout de souffle*', *Le Monde*, 18 March 1960, p. 5 (quoted in English in Dudley, op. cit., p. 182).

18   Louis Marcorelles, *Sight and Sound*, 29 (Spring 1960), p. 85.

19    Gérald Devries, 'À bout de souffle, un début qui fera date', Démocratie 60, 25 March 1960.

20    François Truffaut, 'À bout de souffle', Radio-Cinéma-Télévision, 4 October 1959, p. 54.

21    Ibid., pp. 3, 54.

22    Michèle Manceaux, interview with Godard, in L'Express, 23 December 1959.

23    Ibid.

24    Gilbert Salachas, Radio-Télévision-Cinéma, 3 April 1960, p. 1.

25    Jacques Siclier, 'À bout de souffle, le manifeste de la "Nouvelle Vague"', cited in Brody, op. cit., p. 73.

26    Georges Sadoul, Les Lettres françaises, No. 818, 31 March 1960 (trans. in Graham and Vincendeau, op. cit., p. 232).

27    Raymond Borde, Premier Plan, Nouvelle vague 1962 (quoted in translation from Graham and Vincendeau, op. cit., p. 231).

28    René Cortade, Arts, 23 March 1960.

29    Louis Seguin, Positif, No. 33, April 1960.

30    Borde, Buache and Curtelin, op. cit., p. 64.

31    Luc Moullet, 'Jean-Luc Godard', Cahiers du cinéma, No. 106, April 1960 (trans. in Graham and Vincendeau, op. cit., p. 221).

32    Brosley Crowther, New York Times, 8 February 1961, partly reproduced in Andrew, op. cit., p. 191.

33    Arlene Croce, Film Quarterly 14 (Spring 1961), pp. 54–56, reproduced in Andrew, op. cit., p. 198.

34    Dwight MacDonald, Esquire, July 1961, reprinted in Andrew, op. cit., p. 202.

35    The Times (London), 7 July 1961, in Andrew, op. cit., p. 203.

36    Jim MacBride (10 May 2004) quoted by Brad Stevens, 'The American Friend: Tom Luddy on Jean-Luc Godard', Senses of Cinema, http://archive.sensesofcinema.com/contents/07/44/tom-luddy-godard.html.

37    Jim MacBride quoted by Stephen Farber, in 'A Maverick and a Star Remake the Classic Breathless', Wilmington Morning Star, 22 November 1982, p. 7.

38    Ibid. See also interview with Richard Gere in Karine Signoret, 'Le beau Richard Gere: "Je ne veux pas être un sex symbol"', France-Soir, 6 June 1983.

39    Ibid.

40    Serge Daney, 'Breathless: "Honnête énergie de base"', Libération, 24 June 1983.

41    Vincent Canby, 'Richard Gere in Breathless', New York Times, 13 May 1983. Also available at http://movies.nytimes.com/movie/review?res=9E03EED81138F930A25756C0A965948260.

42    Jeremy Richey, 'Glances At Undervalued Classics: Jim McBride's Breathless (1983)', The Amplifier Online, 6 August, 2008: http://www.bgdailynews.com/articles/2008/08/06/the_amplifier/stage_and_screen/9856undervalued_classics-breathless.txt.

43    Richey, op. cit.

44    Jim MacBride, quoted by Farber, op. cit., p. 7.

45    Canby, op. cit.

46    Richey, op. cit.

47    C.G., 'Un À bout de souffle made in U.S.A. – Jerry Lee Lewis contre Humphrey Bogart', Le Monde, 22 June 1983.

48    Cf. Larissa Macfarquhar, 'In Quentin Tarantino's Mind the Projector Never Stops Running', The New Yorker, Vol. 79, issues 29–33, 20 October, 2003, p. 147. See also Hugh Lloyd, The Rough Guide to Gangster Movies, London: Rough Guides, 2005, p. 56.

49    Richey, op. cit.

50    Jacques Siclier, Nouvelle Vague?, Paris: Éditions du Cerf, 1961, p. 71.

51    Wheeler Winston Dixon, The Films of Jean-Luc Godard, State University of New York, 1997, p. 13.

52    Annette Insdorf, 'A New Direction for the New Wave's Jean-Luc Godard', The New York Times, 12 October 1980, pp. 25, 31; reproduced in David Steritt (ed.), Jean-Luc Godard Interviews, Jackson: University Press of Mississipi, 1998, p. 85.

53    Jacques Richard, 'La Révolution Godard', *Le Figaro*, 31 January 1985.

54    Georges-Marc Benamou, 'Ainsi naquit Jean-Luc Godard …', *Le Quotidien*, 31 January 1985.

55    George Perry in *The Sunday Times*, 24 July 1988 (quoted in Amanda Sheahan Wells, *À bout de souffle*, London: York Press, 2000, p. 81).

56    Alexandre Astruc, 'Le film de Godard fut le coup de foudre, le souffle fou de notre jeunesse …', *VSD*, 16 June 1983.

57    Martyn Auty, 'Breathless *Diva*', *Sight and Sound*, Vol. 51, No. 4, Autumn 1982.

58    'Leos Carax talks about Jean-Luc Godard and David Bowie, silent cinema and working with actors, to David Thompson', in *Sight and Sound*, Vol. 2, No. 5, September 1992.

59    David Thompson, 'Once Upon a Time in Paris', *Sight and Sound*, Vol. 2, No. 5, September 1992.

60    René Predal, *Le Cinéma français depuis 1945*, Paris: Éditions Nathan, 1991, p. 465.

61    Mark Kermode, inside cover of the VHS version of *À bout de souffle*, 1993 (quoted in Wells, op. cit., p. 44).

62    Martial Solal, interview with Stéphane Lerouge, in the booklet accompanying the new release of the musical score on CD: '*À bout de souffle*, musique de Martial Solal, bande originale du film de Jean-Luc Godard', Universal Music Jazz France, 2002.

# Conclusion

The cult status that *À bout de souffle* acquired at its first release and has since managed to uphold places its author among only a handful of 'great *cinéastes* whose debut feature was both their most famous film and their biggest commercial success', as Antoine de Baecque observed in his biography of Godard.[1] Hailed as the New Wave manifesto, and compared by some with Orson Welles's *Citizen Kane* for its revolutionary visual style, *À bout de souffle* marked a radical break away from the codes of classical narration and continuity editing. The unprecedented critical and commercial success of Godard's debut feature can be attributed partly to a number of idiosyncratic authorial markers and partly to an extremely efficient publicity campaign at the time of the film's first release. As the iconoclastic statement of a young *cinéaste* who spent his formative years engaging in debates and writing for *Cahiers du cinéma*, *À bout de souffle* convincingly showed that the new French cinema had the ability to challenge the conventions of popular Hollywood genres by proposing a home-grown radical approach to film narrative and a readily identifiable visual style that could hope to match the box-office returns of American productions in Paris and mainland France. Not surprisingly, film historians and critics have been inclined to associate French national identity (as pitted against the American domination of the market in an increasingly globalised context) with the birth of the *auteur* theory and with its distinctive aesthetics. In commenting on the triumphant selection of Truffaut's *Les Quatre cents coups* to represent France at Cannes in 1959, Godard emphatically aligned himself with the young film buffs and critics, 'those of us – he argued – who on this paper [*Arts*], in *Cahiers du cinéma*, *Positif* or *Cinéma 59*, no matter where, on the back page of *Le Figaro Littéraire* or *France-Observateur* […], those of us who waged, in homage to Louis Delluc, Roger Leenhardt, and André Bazin, the battle for the film *auteur*'.[2] Eventually, the New Wave directors not only entered art history but profoundly altered the perception of filmmaking for generation upon generation of critical observers and practitioners alike. As Jacques Richard remarked in an article entitled 'The Godard Revolution' which greeted the film's second theatrical release in 1985, 'nothing has ever been the same since the 'electroshock' that he [Godard] inflicted on the seventh art'.[3] And the same can be said about a certain American cinema, more specifically about the generation of US independent filmmakers including Martin Scorsese, John Cassavetes, Brian de Palma and Francis Coppola, among others. The 'first-person' cinema pioneered by Truffaut and Godard brought into sharp relief the polemics associated with the *politique des auteurs*. It taught the up and coming American directors of the 1960s that rules were there to be broken and that the autonomy and expediency of a small-budget production, using real locations and a crew reduced to a bare minimum, provided an alternative to the costly studio system. More than any other New Wave debut feature, *À bout de souffle* engaged with the Hollywood codes in an explicit, and occasionally self-reflexive or parodic, manner. Its status as the manifesto of the group reflected the perceived correspondence between the *cinéphile* ideology and the overt acknowledgement of its sources in the film's narrative and complex web of intertextual references. Godard's American biographer, Richard Brody, thus rightly pointed out that:

> All of Godard's friends in the New Wave were deeply affected and influenced by the recent American cinema. However, the first films of the New Wave – those of Chabrol and Truffaut, as well as the early efforts of Rivette and Rohmer – hardly resembled it. [...] Only Godard made a film that in story, in style, and in substance is directly derived from the American movies they admired.[4]

Given, moreover, its inherent concern with filmmaking itself, with the history and the conventions of cinema from its European beginnings to the classical Hollywood era, it is hardly surprising that *À bout de souffle* has never really lost its appeal. After the mitigated success of Jim McBride's remake that marked a rather disappointing return to the Hollywood practices denounced by Godard, *À bout de souffle* continued to inspire young US experimental directors right up to the most recent fifteen-minute remake, *Happiness Is No Fun* (2005), by Brooklyn based *cinéaste* Brandon Harris. More faithful to the editing and acting of the original than its predecessor, *Happiness Is No Fun* adds a political 'black-power' edge to the story that resonates well with Godard's similar denunciation of what Harris calls 'blaxploitation' films such as in *Weekend* (1967) and *One Plus One* a.k.a. *Sympathy for the Devil* (1968).

On the other side of the Atlantic, the iconic status of Godard's meta-narrative film that commented on its own polemical relationship to Hollywood inspired the directors of the so-called *Cinéma du Look*, in particular Jean-Jacques Beineix and Leos Carax, whose work has most often been associated with the advent of postmodernism in French cinema. Beineix's highly successful debut feature, *Diva* (1981), prompted immediate correlations with Godard due to the similar parodic appropriation of the thriller genre, the characters' lack of psychological depth and the emphasis on *mise-en-scène* rather than plot. The release of Carax's $28 million feature *Les Amants du Pont-Neuf* in 1991 was also greeted as the work of a Godard fan, although his first film, *Boy Meets Girl* (1983), displayed the most obvious affinities with the black-and-white experimental aesthetics pioneered in *À bout de souffle*.

In 1995, the Franco-German ARTE television channel broadcast the first feature-length documentary on the making of *À bout de souffle*. Directed by Xavier Villetard and Claude Ventura, *Chambre 12, Hôtel de Suède* includes invaluable first-hand witness accounts, production photographs and interviews that both testify to the film's longevity and heighten the intensely nostalgic mood of the documentary built in part around the imminent disappearance of one of the fetish locations in *À bout de souffle*, the hotel room in which Patricia and Michel have probably the longest conversation in any thriller. Watching *Chambre 12, Hôtel de Suède*, one is reminded of the reasons why the iconoclastic project of an ambitious *cinéaste* ended up as a hugely successful critical and commercial enterprise that not only captured the rebellious spirit of the young French generation of the 1950s but also managed to embody the aesthetic and ideological programme of the *Nouvelle Vague*. If sociologists and film critics recognised in it a sign of the profound changes in mentality that were to shake French society a decade later, aspiring filmmakers on both sides of the Atlantic have never ceased to draw inspiration from its stylistic audacity and self-referential engagement with cinematic conventions.

### Notes

1   Antoine de Baecque, *Godard – biographie*, Paris: Grasset, 2010, p. 111.
2   Jean-Luc Godard, 'Debarred Last Year from the Festival Truffaut will Represent France at Cannes with *Les 400 Coups*', *Arts*, April 1959, reprinted in Milne, op. cit., p. 147.
3   Richard, op. cit.
4   Brody, op. cit., p. 70.

# Appendix 1: Credits

*À bout de souffle* – France, 1960

**Crew:**
**Director:** Jean-Luc Godard
**Production Companies:** Impéria Films, Société de Voucelle de Cinéma
**Producer:** Georges de Beauregard
**Production department (*régie*):** Gaston Dona
**Screenplay and dialogues:** Jean-Luc Godard, based on an original treatment by François Truffaut
**Director of Photography:** Raoul Coutard
**Cameraman:** Claude Beausoleil
**Editor:** Cécile Decugis
**Assistant editor:** Lila Herman
**Assistant director:** Pierre Risient
**Artistic and Technical Advisor:** Claude Chabrol
**Script girl:** Suzanne Faye
**Make-up:** Phuong Maittret
**Sound:** Jacques Maumont
**Still photographers:** Raymond Cauchetier

**Running time:** 87 minutes
**Production format:** 35mm
**Negative and positive film:** [Kodak (black and white)]
**Projection format:** 1 x 1.33
**Locations:** Marseille and Paris
**Shooting Schedule:** 17 August–15 September 1959
**Release date:** 16 March 1960 (Paris); February 1961 (New York)
**Pre-credit text:** Ce film est dédié à la Monogram Pictures [This film is dedicated to Monogram Pictures]

**Cast:**

| | |
|---|---|
| Jean-Paul Belmondo | Michel Poiccard/Laszlo Kovacs |
| Jean Seberg | Patricia Franchini |
| Van Doude | Journalist Van Doude |
| Daniel Boulanger | Detective Vital |
| Henry-Jacques Huet | Antonio Berruti |
| Jean-Pierre Melville | Novelist Parvulesco |
| Richard Balducci | (Luis) Tolmatchoff |
| Roger Hanin | Carl Zumbart/Zombach |
| Claude Mansard | Claudius Mansard (used-car dealer) |
| Liliane David | Liliane, the script girl |
| Michel Fabre | Vital's assistant |
| Jean Domarchi | Mugged man in the toilets |
| Jean Douchet | Driver of the 4CV |
| Jacques Rivette | Man run over by the 4CV |

| André S. Labarthe | Journalist at Orly |
| François Moreuil | Photographer at Orly |
| Jacques Siclier | Journalist at Orly |
| Jean Herman | Soldier who asks Poiccard for a light |
| Jean-Luc Godard | Informer who buys *France-Soir* |

**Brief appearances:** Philippe de Broca, Louigny, René Bernard, Guido Orlando, Jacques Serguine

**Music:** Martial Solal, Mozart's *Clarinet Concerto* K. 622
**Music extract on the radio:** 'Il n'y a pas d'amour heureux' by Georges Brassens

# Appendix 2: Scene Breakdown

**00:00:00 – Title; dedication**
Visa de censure no.. ; dedication: Ce film est dédié à la Monogram Pictures; title: *À bout de souffle* in white letters on black background; music by Martial Solal.

**00:00:15 – Sequence 1: Marseille Harbour. Poiccard steals an American car**
Sun-glassed Michel Poiccard feigns reading the newspaper, while waiting to steal a car. With the help of a young brunette, who beckons him at the right moment, he hot-wires an American car and drives off to Paris, refusing to take her along. Cross-fading. Music.

**00:01:38 – Sequence 2: Driving on the Nationale 7 to Paris**
Michel chatters loudly about his girlfriend, listens to the radio and plays around with a gun he finds in the glove compartment. Failing to stop at a police check, he is chased by two motorcycle cops, swerves into a country road, but is caught up when trying to re-start the engine. He picks up the gun from the glove compartment, fires and kills the cop. He is then seen running away across a barren field. Fade to black. Music.

**00:05:17 – Sequence 3: Early next morning in Paris**
Michel arrives penniless in Paris having hitch-hiked in a 2CV car. He goes into a phone booth to make a call, then buys a newspaper and tries to get some money from Patricia's hotel room while she's out. Next he walks into a café, orders breakfast, but leaves saying he will be back shortly.

**00:06:24 – Sequence 4: The script girl**
[07.02] Michel visits an ex-girlfriend, who works as a television continuity girl. The radio presenter announces: 'It is two minutes past seven'. She first refuses to lend him money then offers him five hundred francs, which he turns down. In the end, Michel steals money from her as she is getting dressed.

**00:09:11 – Sequence 5: The Inter-Americana Agency and the Champs-Élysées [9 mins]**
He unsuccessfully tries to find his friend, Tolmatchoff, at the Agence Interamericana [5']. He then meets Patricia Franchini (Jean Seberg), a young American student and aspiring journalist, who sells the *New York Herald Tribune* on the Champs-Élysées. Michel asks her whether she will accompany him to Rome, and they decide to meet again that evening [3'07']. Michel walks past a cinema poster with the slogan: 'Live dangerously until the end', then comes across a pedestrian (Jacques Rivette) who has just been run over by a 4CV [37']. Back at the Agence Interamericana, Tolmatchoff gives Michel a cheque which, because of his recent troubles, Michel can only cash with the help of another friend, Antonio Berruti. [2'29'] Shortly afterwards, two policemen arrive to question Tolmatchoff. They rush off in Michel's pursuit [1'31']. The publicity of another cinema poster reads: 'The Harder They Fall'. Michel stares intently at photographs of Humphrey Bogart, and mimics his trademark gesture, passing his thumb over his lips [1'10']. Iris shot.

**00:18:12 – Sequence 6: Patricia leaves Michel to meet Van Doude**
He meets up with Patricia and invites her to dinner, although he has no money. Under the pretext of making a phone call, he goes into the toilets of a bar, mugs a man and steals his wallet. Patricia, however, leaves Michel to go to a meeting with an American journalist and discuss the details of an interview at Orly airport. Michel drives her to the Champs-Élysées.

**00:22:39 – Sequence 7: Patricia and Van Doude**
Van Doude offers Patricia a book (Faulkner's *The Wild Palm*), and warns her about the dangers of an unwanted pregnancy. He tells her a story about a girlfriend he forgot to sleep with. They continue to talk, switching occasionally from English to French. Eventually Van Doude mentions Patricia's interview with the novelist Parvulesco due to take place the next day. As they leave, Michel sees Van Doude putting his arm around Patricia's shoulder and kissing her. Night falls over the Champs-Élysées. Fade out.

**00:26:23 – Sequence 8: Patricia's hotel room, next morning**
Patricia returns to her hotel room, only to find that Michel has been waiting for her. A long conversation follows, during which Patricia reveals that she may be pregnant by him. Michel casually dismisses her worries and asks her to make love to him. He tries several times to phone his friend, Antonio. He leaves a message for Mansard, recommending himself as Laszlo Kovacs. Patricia mentions Faulkner's *The Wild Palms*. As the radio presenter announces the broadcast 'Work in Music', Michel and Patricia make love. She then tells Michel it is midday and she has to buy a dress for her interview at Orly. The radio news broadcast mentions President Eisenhower's meeting with President de Gaulle. Michel says he is tired and is going to die. They kiss.

**00:50: 25 – Sequence 9: The informer**
Michel steals a convertible to drive Patricia to Orly. They stop over at the *New York Herald Tribune* offices. While waiting for Patricia in the car, Michel buys *France-Soir* from a street vendor. A man in dark glasses (Jean-Luc Godard) also buys the newspaper, and recognises Michel from the front-page picture. Just as Michel and Patricia drive off, the man goes over to speak to two policemen walking down the street. Iris out and dramatic music.

**00:53:40 – Sequence 10: Interview at Orly**
Patricia takes part in the press conference of the novelist Parvulesco (Jean-Pierre Melville) at Orly. Photographers and journalists fight to get the novelist's attention. Parvulesco answers questions on love, sexuality, infidelity and music in peremptory fashion. Patricia asks him about the role of women in society. The interview ends with Parvulesco's remarks on his greatest ambition in life: 'to become immortal and then to die'. Cross-fading.

**00:57:13 – Sequence 11: The car dealer**
Michel tries to sell the stolen car to a garage in the suburbs, but Mansard, the dealer, refuses and threatens to turn him in to the police. Michel tries once again to call Antonio Berruti, but doesn't find him. Caught rummaging in a drawer in Mansard's office, Michel tries to persuade him to lend him some money. Failing this, he goes over to the car but Mansard has disconnected the distributor wire. Michel is furious and punches Mansard, then steals some money from him for a taxi. Fade out to black.

**00:59:55 – Sequence 12: Police surveillance, cinemas**
Michel and Patricia are trying once again to catch up with Antonio Berruti, but miss him. Next, they head for the offices of the *New York Herald Tribune*. They get off, and Michel tells the driver to wait [2'7']. They cross a courtyard and go through a dark passageway. At the other end they part and Michel tells Patricia he will pick her up later [47']. Van Doude is waiting for Patricia as she arrives at the newspaper offices. Inspector Vital and his assistant arrive shortly afterwards. Vital warns Patricia that she may lose her work permit if she does not collaborate with the police, then hands her a piece of paper with his phone number [2'58']. As Patricia comes out of the newspaper offices, she is followed by Vital's assistant and by Michel. Patricia tries to lose the detective by going into a cinema. She sits down then goes to the women's lavatory and finally escapes by jumping out of a ground-floor window. She meets up with Michel in the street and they decide to go to see a film until nightfall. Fade to black [3'1']. A fade in reveals Michel and Patricia in close up kissing, while a French voice apparently dubbing the soundtrack of the American western can be heard reciting a poem [16']. Fade out.

**01:09:14 – Sequence 13: At Montparnasse with Zumbart and Berruti**
Patricia and Michel come out of the Napoléon film theatre. It is dark [10']. Long shot of a white car pulling up. Patricia jumps out of the car and enters a drugstore. Above the entrance a tele-news marquee announces that the police are closing in on Michel Poiccard [13']. Patricia is reading the latest newspaper headlines as Michel is driving. Michel decides they have to switch cars and goes to a garage [1'12']. Patricia suggests stealing a Cadillac and Michel agrees. She drives past the guard [52']. On top of a building a large tele-news marquee announces Michel's arrest as imminent. They drive down boulevard Saint Germain and Michel is recognised by the script girl (Liliane) from sequence 4 who is reading the newspaper [33']. They arrive at the Pergola, looking for Berruti, but are told he has gone to Montparnasse with Zumbart [33']. They eventually catch up with Berruti who is busy taking photographs in order to blackmail someone [1' 14']. Patricia sees Van Doude and goes with him and an older couple to a café, as Michel talks to Berruti who agrees to cash his cheque for him [40']. Berruti suggests that Michel and Patricia spend the night in the studio of Zumbart's girlfriend. They part and a high-angle shot shows the car going down boulevard Montparnasse. Cut [43'].

**01:15:27 – Sequence 14: The Swedish photographer's studio**
Michel and Patricia arrive at the photographer's studio and watch him work then leave with the model. Patricia puts on a recording of Mozart's *Clarinet Concerto*. Michel tells her that his father played the clarinet. An extreme close-up of his hand holding Maurice Sach's book, *Abracadabra*, reveals a quote on the cover: 'We're all dead men on leave'. Patricia tells him that it's sad to fall asleep because you have to separate: 'They say "sleep together", but it's not true'. Fade to black [1'47'].

**01:17:13 – Sequence 15: Patricia calls the police**
The next morning, Michel asks Patricia to buy *France-Soir* and a bottle of milk. Patricia leaves [1' 2']. She goes past a newsagent's selling lottery tickets, walks into a café where she calls Inspector Vital and tells him where to find Michel [1']. Back in the studio, she warns Michel that she has called the police. He goes out to meet Berruti who arrives in a convertible. Michel refuses Berruti's help yet picks up the gun that Berruti tosses to him as he drives away. Three detectives arrive. Inspector Vital shoots Michel in the back. Patricia runs down the street towards him and looks at him as he pulls the faces he made at her in sequence 8. Just before dying Michel says: 'It's really disgusting'. Patricia asks the policemen what he said. They tell her Michel called her 'disgusting' [*dégueulasse*]. She turns and looks straight into the camera, rubbing her lip as Michel used to do: 'What is *dégueulasse*?' Her theme plays as she stares straight ahead, then turns away from the camera and the back of her head fills the screen. Fade out.

**01:26:05 – The End. No Credits**

# Appendix 3: Filmographies and Awards

*Opération béton* [Operation Concrete], 1955, dir. Jean-Luc Godard
**Script:** Jean-Luc Godard
**Camera:** Adrien Porchet
**Sound:** Jean-Luc Godard
**Editing:** Jean-Luc Godard
**Producer:** Jean-Luc Godard
**Production:** Actua Film
**Format:** 20 min, 35mm, b/w, documentary

*Une femme coquette* [A Flirtatious Woman], 1956, dir. Jean-Luc Godard
**Script:** Hans Lucas (Jean-Luc Godard)
**Camera:** Hans Lucas
**Editing:** Hans Lucas
**Producer:** Jean-Luc Godard
**Cast includes:** Jean-Luc Godard, Maria Lysandre, Roland Tolmatchoff
**Format:** 10 min, 16mm, b/w, short fiction

*Tous les garçons s'appellent Patrick* [All Boys Are Called Patrick], a.k.a
*Charlotte et Véronique*, 1957, dir. Jean-Luc Godard
**Script:** Éric Rohmer
**Camera:** Michel Latouche
**Sound:** Jacques Maumont
**Editing:** Jean-Luc Godard, Cécile Decugis
**Producer:** Pierre Braunberger
**Production:** Les Films de la Pléiade
**Cast includes:** Nicole Berger, Jean-Claude Brialy, Anne Colette
**Format:** 21 min, 35mm, b/w, short fiction

*Une histoire d'eau* [A Story of Water], 1958, dir. Jean-Luc Godard
**Co-director:** François Truffaut
**Script:** Jean-Luc Godard, François Truffaut
**Camera:** Michel Latouche
**Sound:** Jacques Maumont
**Editing:** Jean-Luc Godard
**Producer:** Pierre Braunberger
**Production:** Les Films de la Pléiade
**Cast includes:** Jean-Claude Brialy, Caroline Dim
**Format:** 18 min, 35mm, b/w, short fiction

*Charlotte et son Jules* [Charlotte and Her Boyfriend], 1958, dir. Jean-Luc Godard
**Script:** Jean-Luc Godard
**Camera:** Michel Latouche
**Sound:** Jacques Maumont

**Editing:** Jean-Luc Godard
**Producer:** Pierre Braunberger
**Production:** Les Films de la Pléiade
**Cast includes:** Jean-Paul Belmondo, Gérard Blain, Anne Colette
**Format:** 20 min, 35mm, b/w, short fiction (first distributed in 1961)

*À bout de souffle* [Breathless], 1960, dir. Jean-Luc Godard
Prix Jean Vigo – February 1960

*Le Petit Soldat* [The Little Soldier], 1960, dir. Jean-Luc Godard
**Script:** Jean-Luc Godard
**Camera:** Raoul Coutard
**Editing:** Nadine Marquand, Lila Herman, Agnès Guillemot
**Music:** Maurice Leroux
**Sound:** Jacques Maumont
**Producer:** Georges de Beauregard
**Cast includes:** Michel Subor, Anna Karina, László Szabó
**Format:** 88 min, 35mm, b/w, fiction feature

*Une femme est une femme* [A Woman Is a Woman], 1961, dir. Jean-Luc Godard
**Script:** Jean-Luc Godard, based on an idea from Geneviève Cluny
**Camera:** Raoul Coutard
**Editing:** Agnès Guillemot
**Music:** Michel Legrand
**Art Director:** Bernard Evein
**Sound:** Guy Villette, Jacques Maumont
**Producer:** Georges de Beauregard, Carlo Ponti
**Cast includes:** Anna Karina, Jean-Claude Brialy, Jean-Paul Belmondo, Catherine Demongeot
**Format:** 84 min, 35mm, colour, fiction feature

*La Paresse* [Sloth] – episode in *Les Sept péchés capitaux* [The Seven Deadly Sins], 1962, dir. Jean-Luc Godard
**Script:** Jean-Luc Godard
**Camera:** Henri Decaë
**Editing:** Jacques Gaillard
**Music:** Michel Legrand
**Sound:** Jean-Claude Marchetti
**Producer:** Joseph Bercholz
**Cast includes:** Eddie Constantine, Nicole Mirel
**Format:** 15 min, 35mm, b/w, short fiction

*Vivre sa vie* [It's My Life], 1962, dir. Jean-Luc Godard
**Script:** Jean-Luc Godard
**Camera:** Raoul Coutard
**Editing:** Agnès Guillemot
**Music:** Michel Legrand
**Sound:** Guy Villette
**Producer:** Pierre Braunberger
**Production:** Les Films de la Pléiade
**Cast includes:** Anna Karina, Peter Kassovitz, André S. Labarthe, Brice Parain
**Format:** 90 min, 35mm, b/w, fiction feature

*Le Nouveau Monde* [The New World – episode in *RoGoPaG*], 1963, dir. Jean-Luc Godard
**Script:** Jean-Luc Godard
**Camera:** Jean Rabier
**Editing:** Agnès Guillemot, Lila Lakshmanan
**Sound:** André Hervé
**Producer:** Alfredo Bini
**Production:** Société Lyre Cinématographique/Arco Film/Cineriz
**Cast includes:** Jean-Marc Bory, Michel Delahaye, Jean-André Fieschi, Alexandra Stewart
**Format:** 20 min, 35mm, b/w, short fiction

*Les Carabiniers* [The Riflemen], 1963, dir. Jean-Luc Godard
**Script:** Jean-Luc Godard, Jean Gruault, Roberto Rossellini, based on Carabinieri by Benjamin Joppolo
**Camera:** Raoul Coutard
**Editing:** Agnès Guillemot, Lila Lakshamanan
**Sound:** Jacques Maumont, Bernard Orthion
**Producer:** Georges de Beauregard, Carlo Ponti
**Production:** Rome-Paris Films/Les Films Marceau/Cinor
**Cast includes:** Geneviève Galéa, Albert Juross, Marino Masé, Catherine Ribeiro
**Format:** 80 min, 35mm, b/w, fiction feature

*Le Grand Escroc* [The Great Swindle] – episode in *Les Plus Belles Escroqueries du monde* [World's Greatest Swindles], 1963, dir. Jean-Luc Godard
**Script:** Jean-Luc Godard
**Camera:** Raoul Coutard
**Editing:** Agnès Guillemot
**Music:** Michel Legrand
**Sound:** André Hervé
**Producer:** Pierre Roustang
**Production:** Ulysse Productions/LUX-CCF/Primex Films/Vidès Cinematografica/Toho-Toawa/Cesar Film Productie
**Cast includes:** Charles Denner, Jean Seberg, László Szabó
**Format:** 25 min, 35mm, b/w, short fiction (released 1964)

*Le Mépris* [Contempt], 1963, dir. Jean-Luc Godard
**Script:** Jean-Luc Godard, from the novel *Il disprezzo* by Alberto Moravia
**Camera:** Raoul Coutard
**Sound:** William Sivel
**Editing:** Agnès Guillemot, Lila Lakshmanan
**Producer:** Joseph Levine, Carlo Ponti
**Production:** Rome-Paris Films/Les Films Concordia/Compagnia Cinematografica Champion
**Cast includes:** Brigitte Bardot, Fritz Lang, Jack Palance, Michel Piccoli
**Format:** 110 min, 35mm, colour, fiction feature

*Bande à part* [Band of Outsiders], 1964, dir. Jean-Luc Godard
**Script:** Jean-Luc Godard, based on *Fool's Gold* by Dolores and Bert Hitchens
**Camera:** Raoul Coutard
**Sound:** René Levert, Antoine Bonfanti
**Editing:** Agnès Guillemot, Françoise Collin
**Producer:** jean-Luc Godard
**Production:** Anouchka Films/Orsay Films
**Cast includes:** Claude Brasseur, Anna Karina, Sami Frey, Ernest Menzer
**Format:** 95 min, 35mm, b/w, fiction feature

*Une femme mariée* [The Married Woman], 1964, dir. Jean-Luc Godard
**Script:** Jean-Luc Godard
**Camera:** Raoul Coutard
**Sound:** Antoine Bonfanti, René Levert, Jacques Maumont
**Editing:** Agnès Guillemot, Françoise Collin
**Producer:** Jean-Luc Godard
**Production:** Anouchka Films/Orsay Films
**Cast includes:** Roger Leenhardt, Philippe Leroy, Macha Méril, Bernard Noël
**Format:** 98 min, 35mm, b/w, fiction feature

*Monparnasse-Levallois* [Monparnasse-Levallois] – episode in *Paris vu par ...* [Six in Paris], 1964, dir. Jean-Luc Godard
**Script:** Jean-Luc Godard, based on a story by Jean Giraudoux
**Camera:** Albert Maysles
**Sound:** René Levert
**Editing:** Jackie Raynal
**Producer:** Barbert Schroeder
**Cast includes:** Johanna Shimkus, Philippe Hiquilly, Serge Davri
**Format:** 18 min, 16mm, colour, short fiction

*Alphaville* [Alphaville], 1965, dir. Jean-Luc Godard
**Script:** Jean-Luc Godard
**Camera:** Raoul Coutard
**Sound:** René Levert
**Editing:** Agnès Guillemot
**Producer:** André Michelin
**Production:** Chaumiane/Filmstudio
**Cast includes:** Eddie Constantine, Anna Karina, László Szabó, Akim Tamiroff
**Format:** 98 min, 35mm, b/w, fiction feature

*Pierrot le fou* [Pierrot Goes Wild], 1965 dir. Jean-Luc Godard
**Script:** Jean-Luc Godard, from the novel *Obsession* by Lionel White
**Camera:** Raoul Coutard
**Sound:** René Levert, Antoine Bonfanti
**Editing:** Françoise Collin, Andrée Choty
**Producer:** Georges de Beauregard, Dino de Laurentiis
**Production:** Production Georges de Beauregard/Rome-Paris Films/Dino de Laurentiis Cinematografica
**Cast includes:** Jean-Paul Belmondo, Anna Karina, Dirk Sanders.
**Format:** 110 min, 35mm, colour, fiction feature

*Masculin, féminin* [Masculine, Feminine], 1966 dir. Jean-Luc Godard
**Script:** Jean-Luc Godard, based on *Le Signe* and *La Femme de Paul* by Guy de Maupassant
**Camera:** Willy Kourant
**Sound:** René Levert, Antoine Bonfanti
**Editing:** Agnès Guillemot, Geneviève Bastid
**Producer:** Anatole Dauman
**Production:** Anouchka Films/Argos Films/Svensk Filmindustri/Sandrews
**Cast includes:** Michel Debord, Chantal Goya, Marlène Jobert, Jean-Pierre Léaud
**Format:** 110 min, 35mm, b/w, fiction feature

*Made in USA*, 1966 dir. Jean-Luc Godard
**Script:** Jean-Luc Godard, based on the novel *The Jugger* by Richard Stark
**Camera:** Willy Kourant
**Sound:** René Levert, Jacques Maumont

**Editing:** Agnès Guillemot, Geneviève Letellier
**Producer:** Georges de Beauregard
**Production:** Anouchka Films/Rome-Paris Films/SEPIC
**Cast includes:** Anna Karina, Philippe Labro, László Szabó, Jean-Pierre Léaud
**Format:** 90 min, 35mm, colour, fiction feature

*Deux ou trois choses que je sais d'elle* [Two or Three Things I Know About Her], 1967, dir. Jean-Luc Godard
**Script:** Jean-Luc Godard
**Camera:** Raoul Coutard
**Sound:** René Levert, Antoine Bonfanti
**Editing:** Françoise Collin, Chantal Delattre
**Production:** Anouchka Films/Argos Films/Les Films du Carosse/Parc Film
**Cast includes:** Christophe Bourselier, Blandine Jeanson, Raoul Lévy, Marina Vlady.
**Format:** 90 min, 35mm, colour, fiction feature

*Anticipation, ou L'Amour en l'an 2000* [Love Through the Centuries] – episode in *Le Plus Vieux Métier du monde* [The Oldest Profession], 1966, dir. Jean-Luc Godard
**Script:** Jean-Luc Godard
**Camera:** Pierre Lhomme, Armand Marco
**Editing:** Agnès Guillemot, Geneviève Letellier
**Producer:** Joseph Bergholz
**Production:** Francoriz Films/Les Films Gibé/Rialto Films/Rizzoli Editore
**Cast includes:** Jacques Charrier, Anna Karina, Jean-Pierre Léaud, Marilù Tolo
**Format:** 20 min, 35mm, colour, short fiction

*La Chinoise* [The Chinese Woman], 1967, dir. Jean-Luc Godard
**Script:** Jean-Luc Godard
**Camera:** Raoul Coutard
**Sound:** René Levert, Antoine Bonfanti
**Editing:** Agnès Guillemot, Delphine Desfons
**Production:** Anouchka Films/Les Productions de la Guéville/Athos Films/Parc Films/Simar Films
**Cast includes:** Juliet Berto, Omar Diop, Jean-Pierre Léaud, Anne Wiazemsky
**Format:** 90 min, 35mm, colour, fiction feature

*Caméra œil* [Camera Eye] – episode in *Loin du Vietnam* [Far From Vietnam], 1967, dir. Jean-Luc Godard
**Script:** Jean-Luc Godard
**Camera:** Armand Marco, Alain Levent
**Sound:** Antoine Bonfanti
**Editing:** Chris Marker, Jacqueline Meppiel, Ragnar
**Producer:** Jean-Luc Godard
**Production:** SLON/Sofracima
**Cast includes:** Jean-Luc Godard
**Format:** 15 min, 16mm, colour, essay

*L'Aller et le retour des enfants prodigues. Andate e ritorno dei figli prodighi* a.k.a. *L'Amour* [Love] – episode in *Vangelo 70*, a.k.a. *Amore e Rabbia*, a.k.a. *La Contestation* [Love and Anger], 1967, dir. Jean-Luc Godard
**Script:** Jean-Luc Godard
**Camera:** Armand Marco, Alain Levent
**Sound:** Guy Villette, Antoine Bonfanti
**Editing:** Agnès Guillemot, Delphine Desfons
**Producer:** Carlo Lizzani

**Production:** Castoro Films/Anouchka Films
**Cast includes:** Nino Castelnuovo, Christine Guého, Catherine Jourdon, Paolo Pozzesi
**Format:** 26 min, 35mm, colour, short fiction

*Week-end* [Weekend], 1967 dir. Jean-Luc Godard
**Script:** Jean-Luc Godard
**Camera:** Raoul Coutard
**Sound:** René Levert, Antoine Bonfanti
**Editing:** Agnès Guillemot, Odile Fayot
**Production:** Films Copernic/Ascot Cineraïd/Comacico/Lira Films
**Cast includes:** Mireille Darc, Jean-Pierre Kalfon, Jean-Pierre Léaud, Jean Yanne
**Format:** 95 min, 35mm, colour, fiction feature

*Le Gai savoir* [The Joy of Knowledge], 1968, dir. Jean-Luc Godard
**Script:** Jean-Luc Godard, loosely inspired by Rousseau's *Emile*
**Camera:** Georges Leclerc
**Editing:** Germaine Cohen
**Production:** Originally ORTF, later Anouchka Films/Gambit/Bavaria Atelier
**Cast includes:** Jean-Pierre Léaud, Juliet Berto
**Format:** 95 min, 35mm, colour, essay (first distributed in 1969)

*Ciné-tracts*, 1968
**Camera:** Georges Leclerc
**Editing:** Germaine Cohen
**Production:** Originally ORTF, later Anouchka Films/Gambit/Bavaria Ate;ier
**Cast includes:** Jean-Pierre Léaud, Juliet Berto
**Format:** 95 min, 35mm, colour, essay (first distributed in 1969)

*Un film comme les autres* [A Film Like Any Other], 1968
**Camera:** William Lubtchansky, Jean-Luc Godard
**Editing:** Jean-Luc Godard
**Production:** Anouchka Films
**Cast includes:** Three militant students from Nanterre and two workers from the Flins Renault factory (incorporates footage of May 1968 shot by the ARC group)
**Format:** 100 min, 16mm, colour and b/w, essay (first distributed in 1969)

*One Plus One* a.k.a. *Sympathy for the Devil*, 1968, dir. Jean-Luc Godard
**Script:** Jean-Luc Godard
**Camera:** Tony Richmond
**Sound:** Arthur Bradburn, Derek Ball
**Editing:** Ken Rowles, Agnès Guillemot
**Producer:** Iain Quarrier, Michael Pearson
**Production:** Cupid Productions
**Cast includes:** The Rolling Stones, Frankie Dymon Jnr, Iain Quarrier, Anne Wiazemsky
**Format:** 99 min, 35mm, colour, essay

*One American Movie* a.k.a. *One A.M.*, 1968, dir. Jean-Luc Godard
**Script:** Jean-Luc Godard
**Camera:** Donn Pennebaker, Richard Leacock,Raoul Coutard
**Sound:** Mary Lampson, Robert Leacock, Kate Taylor
**Production:** Leacock-Pennebaker Inc
**Cast includes:** Jefferson Airplane, Eldridge Cleaver, Tom Hayden, Rip Torn
**Format:** Unfinished. A ninety-minute compilation of the footage shot for One A.M. and of a film being shot on the making of *One A.M.*, which was edited by Pennebaker and released as *One P.M.* in 1971.

*British Sounds*, a.k.a. *See You at Mao*, 1969, dir. Jean-Luc Godard and Jean-Henri Roger
Script: Jean-Luc Godard, Jean-Henri Roger
Camera: Charles Stewart
Sound: Fred Sharp
Editing: Christine Aya
Producer: Irving Teitelbaum, Kenith Trodd
Production: Kestrel Productions for London Weekend Television
Cast includes: Michael Lonsdale, students from Oxford and Essex, British Motor Co. production line workers (Cowley, Oxford), militant workers from Dagenham
Format: 52 min, 16mm, colour, essay

*Pravda*, 1969, dir. Jean-Luc Godard, Paul Bourron, Jean-Henri Roger
Script: Groupe Dziga Vertov
Editing: Jean-Luc Godard, Christine Aya
Producer: Claude Nedjar
Production: Centre Européen Cinéma-Radio-Télévision
Format: 58 min, 16mm, colour, essay

*Vent d'est* [Wind From the East, a.k.a. East Wind], 1969, dir. Jean-Luc Godard, Jean-Pierre Gorin, Gérard Martin
Script: Daniel Cohn-Bendit, Jean-Luc Godard, Jean-Pierre Gorin
Camera: Mario Vulpiani
Sound: Antonio Ventura, Carlo Diotalevi
Editing: Christine Aya
Production: CCC/Poli Film/Film Kunst/Anouchka Films
Cast includes: Daniel Cohn-Bendit, Glauber Rocha, Gian Maria Volonte, Anne Wiazemsky
Format: 100 min, 16mm, colour, essay

*Lotte in Italia* [Struggles in Italy], 1970, dir. Jean-Luc Godard, Jean-Pierre Gorin
Script: Groupe Dziga Vertov
Camera: Armand Marco
Sound: Antoine Bonfanti
Editing: Christine Aya
Production: Anouchka Films/Cosmoseion for Radiotelevisione Italiana
Cast includes: Cristina Tullio Altan, Jérôme Hinstin, Paolo Pozzesi, Anne Wiazemsky
Format: 76 min, 16mm, colour, essay

*Vladimir et Rosa* [Vladimir and Rosa], 1971, dir. Jean-Luc Godard, Jean-Pierre Gorin
Script: Groupe Dziga Vertov
Camera: Armand Marco, Gérard Martin
Sound: Antoine Bonfanti
Editing: Christine Aya, Chantal Colomer
Production: Munich Tele-Pool/Grove Press Evergreen Films
Cast includes: Yves Alfonso, Jean-Luc Godard, Jean-Pierre Gorin, Anne Wiazemsky
Format: 103 min, 16mm, colour, essay

*Tout va bien* [All's Well], 1972, dir. Jean-Luc Godard, Jean-Pierre Gorin
Script: Jean-Luc Godard, Jean-Pierre Gorin
Camera: Armand Marco
Sound: Bernard Orthion, Antoine Bonfanti
Editing: Kenout Peltier
Producer: Alain Coiffier, Jean-Luc Godard, Jean-Pierre Rassam
Production: Anouchka Films/Vicco Film/Empire Film
Cast includes: Vittorio Caprioli, Jane Fonda, Yves Montand, Jean Pignol
Format: 95 min, 35mm, colour, fiction feature

*Letter to Jane*, 1972, dir. Jean-Luc Godard, Jean-Pierre Gorin
**Script:** Jean-Luc Godard, Jean-Pierre Gorin
**Camera:** Jean-Luc Godard, Jean-Pierre Gorin
**Editing:** Jean-Luc Godard, Jean-Pierre Gorin
**Producer:** Jean-Luc Godard, Jean-Pierre Gorin
**Format:** 52 min, 16mm, colour, essay

*Ici et ailleurs* [Here and Elsewhere], 1974, dir. Jean-Luc Godard, Anne-Marie Miéville [also including Jean-Pierre Gorin's footage from the abandoned Groupe Dziga Vertov project, *Jusqu'à la victoire*]
**Script:** Jean-Luc Godard, Anne-Marie Miéville
**Camera:** William Lubtchansky (Armand Marco for the original *Jusqu'à la victoire*)
**Editing:** Jean-Luc Godard, Anne-Marie Miéville
**Producer:** Jean-Luc Godard, Anne-Marie Miéville, Jean-Pierre Rassam
**Production:** Sonimage/INA/Gaumont
**Cast includes:** Jean-Pierre Bamberger
**Format:** 50 min, 16mm, colour, essay (first distributed in 1976)

*Numéro deux* [Number Two], 1975, dir. Jean-Luc Godard
**Script:** Jean-Luc Godard, Anne-Marie Miéville
**Camera:** William Lubtchansky (film), Gérard Martin (video)
**Technicians:** Milka Assaf, Gérard Martin, Gérard Teissedre
**Sound:** Jean-Pierre Ruh
**Editing:** Jean-Luc Godard, Anne-Marie Miéville
**Producer:** Georges de Beauregard, Jean-Pierre Rassam
**Production:** Sonimage/Bela/SNC
**Cast includes:** Sandrine Battistella, Pierre Oudry, Alexandre Rignault, Rachel Stefanopoli
**Format:** 88 min, 35mm and video, colour, fiction feature

*Six fois deux (Sur et sous la communication)* [Six Times Two (On and Under Communication)], 1976, dir. Jean-Luc Godard, Anne-Marie Miéville
**Script:** Jean-Luc Godard, Anne-Marie Miéville
**Camera:** William Lubtchansky, Dominique Chapuis
**Technicians:** Henri False, Joël Mellier, Philippe Rony, Gérard Teissedre
**Editing:** Jean-Luc Godard, Anne-Marie Miéville
**Producer:** Michel Raux, Jean-Luc Godard
**Production:** Sonimage/INA for FR3
**Format:** 12x50 min, video, colour, 12-episode television series

*Faut pas rêver* [Dream On], 1978, dir. Jean-Luc Godard
**Camera:** Jean-Luc Godard
**Editing:** Jean-Luc Godard, Anne-Marie Miéville
**Cast includes:** 'Camille', voice of Anne-Marie Miéville
**Format:** 2 min, video, colour (illustration of a Patrick Juvet song, broadcast in 1978 on the programme *On ne manque pas d'airs*)

*France/tour/détour/deux/enfants* [France/Tour/Detour/Two/Children], 1979, dir. Jean-Luc Godard, Anne-Marie Miéville
**Script:** Jean-Luc Godard, Anne-Marie Miéville, loosely based on G Bruno's *Le Tour de la France par deux enfants: devoir et patrie* (1884)
**Camera:** William Lubtchansky, Dominique Chapuis, Philippe Rony
**Technicians:** Pierre Binggeli
**Editing:** Jean-Luc Godard, Anne-Marie Miéville
**Production:** Sonimage/INA for Antenne 2

**Cast includes:** Betty Berr, Albert Dray, Arnaud Martin, Camille Virolleaud
**Format:** 12x26 min, video, colour, 12-episode television series

*Scénario vidéo de* Sauve qui peut (la vie) [Video Scenario for *Sauve qui peut (la vie)*], 1979, dir. Jean-Luc Godard
**Script:** Jean-Luc Godard
**Editing:** Jean-Luc Godard
**Production:** Sonimage/Télévision Suisse Romande
**Cast includes:** photographs of Isabelle Huppert, Miou-Miou, Werner Herzog
**Format:** 20 min, video, colour, essay

*Sauve qui peut (la vie)* [Every Man for Himself], 1980, dir. Jean-Luc Godard
**Script:** Jean-Claude Carrière, Anne-Marie Miéville
**Camera:** Renata Berta, William Lubtchansky, Jean-Bernard Menoud
**Sound:** Jacques Maumont, Luc Yersin, Oscar Stellavox
**Editing:** Jean-Luc Godard, Anne-Marie Miéville
**Producer:** Jean-Luc Godard, Alain Sarde
**Production:** Sara Films/MK2/Saga Productions/Sonimage/CNC/ZDF/SSR/ORF
**Cast includes:** Nathalie Baye, Jacques Dutronc, Isabelle Huppert, Cécile Tanner
**Format:** 87 min, 35mm, colour, fiction feature

*Passion, le travail et l'amour: introduction à un scénario*, a.k.a. troisième état du film *Passion* [Passion, The Work and Love: Introduction to a Script], 1981, dir. Jean-Luc Godard
**Script:** Jean-Luc Godard
**Editing:** Jean-Luc Godard
**Production:** Sonimage
**Cast includes:** Jean-Claude Carrière, Isabelle Huppert, Jerzy Radziwilowicz, Hanna Schygulla
**Format:** 30 min, video, colour, essay

*Lettre à Freddy Buache* [Letter to Freddy Buache], 1982, dir. Jean-Luc Godard
**Script:** Jean-Luc Godard
**Camera:** Jean-Bernard Menoud
**Sound:** François Musy
**Editing:** Jean-Luc Godard
**Production:** Sonimage/Film et Vidéo Production Lausanne
**Cast includes:** Jean-Luc Godard
**Format:** 11 min, video transferred to 35mm, colour, essay

*Passion*, 1982, dir. Jean-Luc Godard
**Script:** Jean-Luc Godard
**Camera:** Raoul Coutard
**Editing:** Jean-Luc Godard
**Producer:** Alain Sarde
**Production:** Sara Films/Sonimage/Films A2/Film et Vidéo Production SA/SSR Télévision Suisse
**Cast includes:** Isabelle Huppert, Michel Piccoli, Jerzy Radziwilowicz, Hanna Schygulla
**Format:** 87 min, 35mm, colour, fiction feature

*Scénario du film* Passion [Scenario of the Film *Passion*], 1982, dir. Jean-Luc Godard
**Script:** Jean-Luc Godard
**Collaboration:** Anne-Marie Miéville, Pierre Binggeli, Jean-Bernard Menoud
**Production:** Télévision Romande, JLG Films
**Cast includes:** Jean-Luc Godard, Isabelle Huppert, Jerzy Radziwilowicz, Hanna Schygulla
**Format:** 54 min, video, colour, essay

*Changer d'image*, a.k.a. *Lettre à la bien-aimée* [Change of Image] – episode in *Le Changement à plus d'un titre* [Change in More Than Name], 1982, dir. Jean-Luc Godard
**Script:** Jean-Luc Godard
**Production:** INA/Sonimage
**Cast includes:** Jean-Luc Godard, Jacques Probst, voice of Anne-Marie Miéville
**Format:** 10 min, video, colour, essay

*Prénom Carmen* [First Name Carmen], 1983, dir. Jean-Luc Godard
**Script:** Anne-Marie Miéville
**Camera:** Raoul Coutard
**Sound:** François Musy, Oscar Stellavox
**Editing:** Jean-Luc Godard, Suzanne Lang-Villar
**Producer:** Alain Sarde
**Production:** Sara Films/JLG Films/Films A2
**Cast includes:** Jacques Bonnaffé, Maruschka Detmers, Hyppolite Girardot, Myriem Roussel
**Format:** 84 min, 35mm, colour, fiction feature

*Petites Notes à propos du film* **Je vous salue Marie** [Little Notes on the Film *Je vous salue Marie*], 1983, dir. Jean-Luc Godard
**Script:** Jean-Luc Godard
**Camera:** Jean-Luc Godard
**Editing:** Jean-Luc Godard
**Production:** JLG Films
**Cast includes:** Jean-Luc Godard, Myriem Roussel, Thierry Rode, Anne-Marie Miéville
**Format:** 25 min, video, colour, essay

*Je vous salue, Marie* [Hail Mary], 1985, dir. Jean-Luc Godard
**Script:** Jean-Luc Godard
**Camera:** François Musy
**Sound:** François Musy, Oscar Stellavox
**Editing:** Jean-Luc Godard
**Production:** Pégasse Films/JLG Films/Sara Films/Channel 4/Gaumont/SSR Télévision Suisse Romande
**Cast includes:** Juliette Binoche, Philippe Lacoste, Thierry Rode, Myriem Roussel
**Format:** 72 min, 35mm, colour, fiction feature

*Détective*, 1985, dir. Jean-Luc Godard
**Script:** Anne-Marie Miéville, Alain Sarde, Philippe Setbon
**Camera:** Bruno Nuytten
**Sound:** François Musy, Pierre Gamet
**Editing:** Marilyne Dubreuil
**Producer:** Alain Sarde
**Production:** Sara Films/JLG Films
**Cast includes:** Nathalie Baye, Claude Brasseur, Alain Cuny, Johnny Hallyday
**Format:** 95 min, 35mm, colour, fiction feature

*Soft and Hard* [Soft Talk on a Hard Subject Between Two Friends], 1985, dir. Jean-Luc Godard, Anne-Marie Miéville
**Script:** Jean-Luc Godard, Anne-Marie Miéville
**Video:** Pierre Binggeli
**Editing:** Jean-Luc Godard, Anne-Marie Miéville
**Producer:** Tony Kirkhope
**Production:** JLG Films/Deptford Beach Productions for Channel 4
**Cast includes:** Jean-Luc Godard, Anne-Marie Miéville
**Format:** 52 min, video, colour, essay

*Grandeur et décadence d'un petit commerce de cinéma* [Grandeur and Decadence of a Small-Time Filmmaker, a.k.a. The Rise and Fall of a Small Film Company], 1986, dir. Jean-Luc Godard
**Script:** Jean-Luc Godard, from the novel *The Soft Centre* by James Hadley Chase.
**Camera:** Caroline Champetier
**Sound:** François Musy, Pierre-Alain Besse
**Editing:** Jean-Luc Godard
**Producer:** Pierre Grimblat
**Production:** Hampster Productions/TF1/Télévision Suisse Romande/RTL/JLG Films
**Cast includes:** Jean-Luc Godard, Jean-Pierre Léaud, Jean-Pierre Mocky, Marie Valéra
**Format:** 90 min, video, colour, telefilm (broadcast in the 'Série Noire' series on TF1 in May 1986)

*Meeting WA* a.k.a. *Meeting Woody Allen*, 1986, dir. Jean-Luc Godard
**Script:** Jean-Luc Godard
**Sound:** François Musy
**Editing:** Jean-Luc Godard
**Production:** JLG Films
**Cast includes:** Jean-Luc Godard, Woody Allen, voice of Annette Insdorf
**Format:** 26 min, video, colour, essay

*Armide* (episode in *Aria*), 1987, dir. Jean-Luc Godard
**Script:** Jean-Luc Godard
**Camera:** Caroline Champetier
**Sound:** François Musy
**Editing:** Jean-Luc Godard
**Producer:** Don Boyd
**Production:** Boyd's Company/Lightyear Entertainment/RVP Productions/Virgin Vision
**Cast includes:** Valérie Alain, Luke Corre, Jacques Neuville, Marion Petersen
**Format:** 12 min, 35mm, colour, short fiction

*Soigne ta droite* [Keep Your Right Up], 1987, dir. Jean-Luc Godard
**Script:** Jean-Luc Godard
**Camera:** Caroline Champetier
**Sound:** François Musy
**Editing:** Jean-Luc Godard, Ruth Waldburger
**Producer:** Jean-Luc Godard, Ruth Waldburger
**Production:** Gaumont/JLG Films/Xanadu Films/RTSR
**Cast includes:** Jane Birkin, Michel Galabru, Les Rita Mitsouko, Jacques Villeret
**Format:** 81 min, 35mm, colour, fiction feature

*King Lear*, 1987, dir. Jean-Luc Godard
**Script:** Jean-Luc Godard
**Camera:** Sophie Maintigneaux
**Sound:** François Musy
**Editing:** Jean-Luc Godard
**Producer:** Yoram Globus, Menahem Golan
**Production:** Cannon
**Cast includes:** Woody Allen, Burgess Meredith, Molly Ringwald, Peter Sellars
**Format:** 90 min, 35mm, colour, fiction feature

*Closed*, 1988, dir. Jean-Luc Godard
**Camera:** Caroline Champetier
**Sound:** François Musy
**Editing:** Jean-Luc Godard
**Production:** JLG Films/Marithé et François Girbaud Design

Cast includes: Girbaud model Keshi, Suzanne Lanza, Luca, Marc Parent
Format: 10x15 sec, video, colour, television advertisements

*On s'est tous défilé* [We All Stole Away], 1988, dir. Jean-Luc Godard
Script: Jean-Luc Godard
Camera: Caroline Champetier
Sound: François Musy
Editing: Jean-Luc Godard
Production: Marithé and François Girbaud Design
Cast includes: Marithé and François Girbaud models presenting the 1988 MFG collection
Format: 13 min, video, colour, essay

*Puissance de la parole* [The Power of Words], 1988, dir. Jean-Luc Godard
Script: Jean-Luc Godard
Camera: Caroline Champetier
Sound: François Musy, Pierre Binggeli
Editing: Jean-Luc Godard
Production: Gaumont/JLG Films/France Télécom
Cast includes: Lydia Andréi, Jean Brouise, Laurence Côte, Jean-Michel Iribarren
Format: 25 min, video, colour, essay

*Le Dernier Mot* [The Last Word] – episode in *Les Français vu par...* [The French Seen By ...],
1988, dir. Jean-Luc Godard
Script: Jean-Luc Godard
Camera: Pierre Binggeli
Sound: Pierre Camus, François Musy
Editing: Jean-Luc Godard
Producer: Anne-Marie Miéville
Production: Erato Films/Socpresse/JLG Films/Le Figaro magazine/Antenne 2
Cast includes: André Marcon, Hans Zischler, Catherine Aymerie, Pierre Amoyal
Format: 12 min, video, colour, short fiction

*Histoires du cinéma* [initial versions of chapters 1A, *Toutes les histoires* (All the Histories) and
1B, *Une histoire seule* (A Solitary Story)], 1989, dir. Jean-Luc Godard
Script: Jean-Luc Godard
Video: Pierre Binggeli
Sound: Jean-Luc Godard, Pierre-Alain Besse, François Musy
Editing: Jean-Luc Godard
Producer: Jean-Luc Godard, Ruth Waldburger
Production: CNC/Canal Plus/La Sept/FR3/Gaumont/JLG Films/Vega Films/RTSR
Format: 2x52 min, video, colour, essay

*Le Rapport Darty* [The Darty Report], 1989, dir. Jean-Luc Godard, Anne-Marie Miéville
Script: Jean-Luc Godard, Anne-Marie Miéville
Camera: Hervé Duhamel
Sound: Pierre-Alain Besse, François Musy
Editing: Jean-Luc Godard, Anne-Marie Miéville
Production: Gaumont/JLG Films
Cast includes: voices of Jean-Luc Godard and Anne-Marie Miéville
Format: 50 min, video, colour, essay

*Nouvelle Vague* [New Wave], 1990, dir. Jean-Luc Godard
Script: Jean-Luc Godard
Camera: William Lubtchansky

**Sound:** Pierre-Alain Besse, Pierre Morelle, François Musy
**Editing:** Jean-Luc Godard
**Producer:** Alain Sarde
**Production:** Sara Films/Périphéria/CNC/Canal Plus/Télévision Suisse Romande/Antenne 2/DFI/ Sofica Investimage/Sofica Creations/Véga Films
**Cast includes:** Alain Delon, Domiziana Giordano, Roland Amstutz, Laurence Côte
**Format:** 89 min, 35mm, colour, fiction feature

*L'Enfance de l'art* [The Childhood of Art] – episode in *Comment vont les enfants* [How Are the Kids?], 1991, dir. Jean-Luc Godard, Anne-Marie Miéville
**Script:** Jean-Luc Godard, Anne-Marie Miéville
**Camera:** Sophie Maintigneux
**Sound:** Pierre-Alain Besse
**Editing:** Jean-Luc Godard
**Production:** JLG Films/UNICEF
**Cast includes:** Nathalie Kadem, Antoine Reyes, Michel Boupoil, Denis Vallas
**Format:** 8 min, 35mm, colour, essay

*Allemagne année 90 neuf zéro* [Germany Year 90 Nine Zero], 1991, dir. Jean-Luc Godard
**Script:** Jean-Luc Godard
**Camera:** Christophe Pollock
**Sound:** Pierre-Alain Besse, François Musy
**Editing:** Jean-Luc Godard
**Producer:** Nicole Ruelle
**Production:** Antenne 2/Brainstorm/Gaumont/Périphéria
**Cast includes:** Eddie Constantine, Hanns Zischler, Claudia Michelsen, Nathalie Kadem
**Format:** 62 min, 35mm, colour, essay

*Pour Thomas Wainggai* [For Thomas Wainggai] – episode in *Écrire contre l'oubli* [Against Oblivion], 1991, dir. Jean-Luc Godard, Anne-Marie Miéville
**Script:** Jean-Luc Godard, Anne-Marie Miéville
**Camera:** Jean-Marc Fabre
**Sound:** Pierre-Alain Besse, François Musy
**Editing:** Jean-Luc Godard
**Production:** Amnesty International PRI/Vega Film
**Cast includes:** André Rousselet, Véronique Tillmann
**Format:** 3 min, video, colour, documentary

*Hélas pour moi* [Oh, Woe Is Me], 1993, dir. Jean-Luc Godard
**Script:** Jean-Luc Godard
**Camera:** Caroline Champetier
**Sound:** François Musy, Pierre-Alain Besse
**Editing:** Jean-Luc Godard
**Producer:** Alain Sarde
**Production:** Vega Films/Les Films Alain Sarde/Canal Plus/Télévision Suisse Romande/ Périphéria
**Cast includes:** Marc Betton, Roland Blanche, Gérard Depardieu, Laurence Masliah
**Format:** 84 min, 35mm, colour, fiction feature

*Les Enfants jouent à la Russie* [The Kids Play Russian], 1993, dir. Jean-Luc Godard
**Script:** Jean-Luc Godard
**Camera:** Caroline Champetier
**Sound:** Stéphane Thiébaud
**Editing:** Jean-Luc Godard

Producer: Alessandro Cecconi, Ira Barmak, Ruth Waldburger
Production: Worldvision Enterprises (N.Y.)/Cecco Films/RTR/Vega Films/JLG Films
Cast includes: Bernard Eisenschitz, Jean-Luc Godard, André S. Labarthe, László Szabó
Format: 63 min, video, colour, essay

*Je vous salue, Sarajevo* [Hail, Sarajevo], 1993, dir. Jean-Luc Godard
Script: Jean-Luc Godard, Anne-Marie Miéville
Editing: Jean-Luc Godard
Format: 2 min, video, colour, essay

*JLG/JLG: autoportrait de décembre* [JLG/JLG Self-Portrait in December], 1995, dir. Jean-Luc Godard
Script: Jean-Luc Godard
Camera: Yves Pouliguen
Sound: Pierre-Alain Besse
Editing: Jean-Luc Godard, Catherine Cormon
Production: Périphéria/Gaumont
Cast includes: Jean-Luc Godard, Denis Jadot, André S. Labarthe, Geneviève Pasquier
Format: 62 min, 35mm, colour, essay

*2x50 ans de cinéma français* [2x50 Years of French Cinema], 1995, dir. Jean-Luc Godard, Anne-Marie Miéville
Script: Jean-Luc Godard, Anne-Marie Miéville
Camera: Isabelle Czajka
Sound: Stéphane Thiebaud
Editing: Jean-Luc Godard
Producer: Colin MacCabe, Bob Last
Production: British Film Institute/Périphéria
Cast includes: Jean-Luc Godard, Estelle Grynspan, Michel Piccoli, Cécile Regnier
Format: 49 min, video, colour, essay

*For Ever Mozart*, 1996, dir. Jean-Luc Godard
Script: Jean-Luc Godard
Camera: Christophe Pollock
Sound: François Musy
Editing: Jean-Luc Godard
Producer: Alain Sarde
Production: Avventura Films/Vega Films/Canal Plus/CEC Rhône-Alpes/France 2 Cinéma/CNC/TSR/Périphéria/Eurimages/DFI/ECM Records
Cast includes: Bérangère Allaux, Madeleine Assas, Ghalya Lacroix, Vicky Messica
Format: 85 min, 35mm, colour, fiction feature

*Adieu au TNS* [Farewell to the Théatre National de Strasbourg], 1996, dir. Jean-Luc Godard
Editing: Jean-Luc Godard
Production: Périphéria
Cast: Jean-Luc Godard
Format: 7 min, video, colour, essay

*Plus Oh!* a.k.a. *Plus haut!* [Higher Still], 1996, dir. Jean-Luc Godard
Editing: Jean-Luc Godard
Production: M6
Cast: France Gall
Format: 6 min, video, colour, music video

*Histoires du cinéma* [Histories of the Cinema], 1998, dir. Jean-Luc Godard
Script: Jean-Luc Godard
Editing: Jean-Luc Godard
Production: Gaumont/Périphéria
Cast includes: Juliette Binoche, Alain Cuny, Serge Daney, Julie Delpy
Format: 214 min, video, colour, 8-part series of essays

*The Old Place*, 1999, dir. Jean-Luc Godard, Anne-Marie Miéville
Script: Jean-Luc Godard, Anne-Marie Miéville
Editing: Jean-Luc Godard, Anne-Marie Miéville
Producer: Mary Lea Bandy, Colin MacCabe
Production: Museum of Modern Art New York/Périphéria
Cast includes: Bérangère Allaux, Madeleine Assas, Ghalya Lacroix, Vicky Messica
Format: 49 min, video, colour, essay

*L'Origine du vingt et unième siècle* [The Origin of the Twenty-First Century], 2000, dir. Jean-Luc Godard
Script: Jean-Luc Godard
Camera: Julien Hirsch
Sound: François Musy
Editing: Jean-Luc Godard
Production: Canal Plus/Véga Films
Format: 15 min, video, colour, essay

*Eloge de l'amour* [In Praise of Love], 2001, dir. Jean-Luc Godard
Script: Jean-Luc Godard
Camera: Julien Hirsch, Christophe Pollock
Sound: François Musy, Christian Monheim
Editing: Jean-Luc Godard
Producer: Alain Sarde, Ruth Waldburger
Production: Avventura Films/Périphéria/Canal Plus/ARTE/Véga Films/TSR
Cast includes: Bruno Putzulu, Cécile Camp, Jean Davy, Françoise Verny
Format: 98 min, 35mm and video, b/w and colour, fiction feature

*Dans le noir du temps* [In The Darkness of Time] – episode in *Ten Minutes Older: The Cello*, 2002, dir. Jean-Luc Godard
Script: Anne-Marie Miéville
Camera: Julien Hirsch
Sound: François Musy
Editing: Jean Luc Godard, Anne-Marie Miéville
Song: Anne-Marie Miéville
Producer: Ulrich Felsberg, Nicolas McClintock, Nigel Thomas
Production: Matador Pictures/Périphéria/Road Movies
Format: 10 min, video, colour, essay

*Liberté et patrie* [Freedom and Fatherland], 2002, dir. Jean-Luc Godard, Anne-Marie Miéville
Script: Jean-Luc Godard, Anne-Marie Miéville
Producer: Ruth Waldburger
Production: Vega Films/Périphéria
Format: 16 min, video, colour, short fiction

*Notre musique* [Our Music], 2004, dir. Jean-Luc Godard
Script: Jean-Luc Godard

**Camera:** Julien Hirsch
**Sound:** François Musy
**Editing:** Jean-Luc Godard
**Producer:** Ruth Waldburger, Jean-Paul Battaggia
**Production:** Avventura Films/Les Films Alain Sarde/Périphéria/France 3 Cinéma/Canal Plus/ TSR/Véga Films
**Cast includes:** Nade Dieu, Rony Kramer, Sarah Adler, Jean-Christophe Bouvet, Mahmoud Darwish, Juan Goytisolo, Alain Bergounioux
**Format:** 80 min, 35mm, colour, fiction feature

*Moments choisis des histoire(s) du cinéma* [Best Moments of Histories of Cinema], 2004, dir. Jean-Luc Godard
**Script:** Jean-Luc Godard
**Editing:** Jean-Luc Godard
**Production:** Gaumont
**Format:** 84 min, video transferred on 35mm, colour, essay

*Prière pour refuzniks* [Prayer for Refuzniks], 2004, dir. Jean-Luc Godard
**Editing:** Jean-Luc Godard
**Production:** Périphéria
**Format:** 7 min, video, essay

*Vrai faux passeport* [Real Faked Passport], 2006, dir. Jean-Luc Godard
**Editing:** Jean-Luc Godard
**Producer:** Jean-Luc Godard
**Production:** Centre Georges Pompidou
**Format:** 55 min, video, essay

*Ecce homo*, 2006, dir. Jean-Luc Godard
**Editing:** Jean-Luc Godard
**Production:** Centre Georges Pompidou
**Format:** 2 min, video, essay

*Une bonne à tout faire* [Maid-of-All-Work], 2006, dir. Jean-Luc Godard
**Editing:** Jean-Luc Godard
**Production:** Centre Georges Pompidou
**Format:** 8 min, video, essay

*Une catastrophe* [A Tragedy], 2008, dir. Jean-Luc Godard
**Editing:** Jean-Luc Godard
**Production:** Viennale
**Format:** 1 min, 35mm, b/w and colour, essay

*Tribute to Éric Rohmer* [Best Moments of Histories of Cinema], 2010, dir. Jean-Luc Godard
**Editing:** Jean-Luc Godard
**Production:** Les Films du Losange
**Cast includes:** Jean-Luc Godard
**Format:** 3 min, video, essay

*Socialisme* [Socialism], 2010, dir. Jean-Luc Godard, Fabrice Aragno, Jean-Paul Battaggia, Paul Grivas
**Script:** Jean-Luc Godard
**Camera:** Julien Hirsch
**Sound:** François Musy, Gabriel Hafner

**Editing:** Jean-Luc Godard
**Producer:** Ruth Waldburger, Jean-Paul Battaggia
**Production:** Vega Films/Office Fédéral de la Culture/TSR/La Ville de Genève/Suissimage/Fondation Vaudoise/Fonds Regio Films/Wild Bunch/Canal Plus
**Cast includes:** Patti Smith, Christian Sinniger, Alain Badiou, Catherine Tanvier, Elias Sanbar
**Format:** 101 min, 35mm, colour, fiction feature

# Appendix 4: Bibliography

Andrew, Dudley (ed.), *Breathless: Jean-Luc Godard, director*, New Brunswick and London: Rutgers University Press, 1990.

Astruc, Alexandre, 'The Birth of a New Avant-Garde: La Caméra-Stylo', in Ginette Vincendeau and Peter Graham (eds), *The New Wave. Critical Landmarks*, pp. 31–37, trans. from *L'Écran français* 144, 30 March 1948.

Astruc, Alexandre, 'Le film de Godard fut le coup de foudre, le souffle fou de notre jeunesse ...', *VSD*, 16 June 1983.

Auty, Martyn, 'Breathless *Diva*', *Sight and Sound*, Vol. 51, No. 4, Autumn 1982.

Baecque, Antoine de, *Godard – biographie*, Paris: Éditions Grasset and Fasquelle, 2010.

Baecque, Antoine de and Toubiana, Serge, *Truffaut*, trans. Catherine Temerson, Berkeley/Los Angeles: University of California Press, 2000.

Barr, Charles, '*À bout de souffle*', in Ian Cameron (ed.), *The Films of Jean-Luc Godard*, New York: Praeger Publishers, 1970.

Barr, Charles, '*À bout de souffle*', in Dudley Andrews (ed.), *Breathless: Jean-Luc Godard, Director*, New Brunswick and London: Rutgers University Press, 1990, pp. 220–223.

Barr Charles, et al., *The Films of Jean-Luc Godard*, New York: Praeger, 1970.

Beau, Frank, 'L'autodafé du carton-pâte', *Cahiers du cinéma* special issue hors série 'Nouvelle Vague, une légende en question', 1998.

Beauregard, Chantal de, *Georges de Beauregard: Premier sourire de Belmondo ... dernier de Bardot*, Paris: Lacour/Colporteur, 1991.

Benamou, Georges-Marc 'Ainsi naquit Jean-Luc Godard ...', *Le Quotidien*, 31 January 1985.

Bergala, Alain (ed.), *Jean-Luc Godard par Jean-Luc Godard*, Paris: Éditions de l'Étoile/Cahiers du Cinéma, 1985.

Bergala, Alain, 'Techniques de la Nouvelle Vague', *Cahiers du cinéma* special issue hors série 'Nouvelle Vague, une légende en question', 1998.

Bessèges, André *France Catholique*, 25 March, 1960.

Borde, Raymond, Buache, Freddy and Curtelin, Jean, *Nouvelle Vague*, SERDOC Imprimerie Molière, 1962.

Bordwell, David, *Narration in the Fiction Film*, London: Methuen, 1985.

Bordwell, David, Staiger, Janet and Thompson, Kristin, *The Classical Hollywood Cinema: Film Style and Mode of Production to 1960*, London: Routledge, 1985.

Boussinot, Roger, *L'Encyclopédie du cinéma*, Paris: Bordas, 1967.

Braunberger, Pierre, *Cinémamémoire*, with a preface by Jean-Luc Godard, Paris: Centre Georges Pompidou/CNC, 1987.

Brody, Richard, *Everything is Cinema: The Working Life of Jean-Luc Godard*, London: Faber and Faber, 2008.

Cameron Ian (ed.), *The Films of Jean-Luc Godard*, New York: Frederick A. Praeger Inc., 1970.

Canby, Vincent, 'Richard Gere in *Breathless*', *New York Times*, 13 May 1983.

Capdenat, Constance, 'Les Enfants terribles de la nouvelle vague', *Vingtième Siècle. Revue d'histoire*, Vol. 22, No. 1, 1989, pp. 45–51.

Cerisuelo, Marc, *Jean-Luc Godard*, Paris: Éditions des Quatre-Vents, 1989.

C.G., 'Un *À bout de souffle made in U.S.A.* – Jerry Lee Lewis contre Humphrey Bogart', *Le Monde*, 22 June 1983.

Charensol, G., '*À bout de souffle* du côté de Hollywood ', *Les Nouvelles littéraires*, 24 March 1960.

Collet, Jean, *Jean-Luc Godard*, Paris: Seghers, 1963.

Collet, Jean, *Jean-Luc Godard: An Investigation into His Films and Philosophy*, trans. by Ciba Vaughan, New York: Crown Publishers Inc., 1970.

Cortade, René, *Arts*, 23 March, 1960.

Courtade, Francis, *Les Malédictions du cinéma français. Une histoire du cinéma français parlant (1928–1978)*, preface by Raymond Borde, Paris: Éditions Alain Moreau, 1978.

Coutard, Raoul, 'La Forme du jour', *Nouvel Observateur*, 22 September 1965, pp. 36–37.

Daney, Serge, '*Breathless*: "Honnête énergie de base"', *Libération*, 24 June 1983.

Daney, Serge and Oudard, Jean-Pierre, 'Le Nom-de-l'Auteur', *Cahiers du cinéma*, No. 234–235, December 1971/January–February 1972.

Darke, Chris, *Alphaville*, London/New York: I.B.Tauris, 2005.

Devries, Gérald, '*À bout de souffle*, un début qui fera date', *Démocratie 60*, 25 March 1960.

Dixon, Wheeler Winston, *The Films of Jean-Luc Godard*, Albany: State University of New York Press, 1997.

Durant, Philippe, *Belmondo*, Lausanne: Pierre-Marcel Favre, 1987.

Esquenazi, Jean-Pierre, *Godard et la société française des années 1960*, Paris: Armand Colin, 2004.

Fabe, Marilyn, 'Film and Postmodernism: Woody Allen's *Annie Hall*', in *Closely Watched Films. An Introduction to the Art of Narrative Film Technique*, Berkley/Los Angeles/London: University of California Press, 2004.

Farber, Stephen, 'A Maverick and a Star Remake the Classic *Breathless*', *Wilmington Morning Star*, 22 November 1982.

Godard, Jean-Luc, *Introduction à une véritable histoire du cinéma*, Paris: Éditions Albatros, 1980.

Godard, Jean-Luc, *Godard par Godard*, edited by Bergala, Alain, Paris: Éditions de l'Étoile/ Cahiers du cinéma, 1985.

Godard, Jean-Luc, *Interviews*, University Press of Mississippi/Jackson, 1998.

Graham, Peter and Vincendeau, Ginette (eds), *The French New Wave: Critical Landmarks*, London: Bfi/Palgrave Macmillan, 2009.

Guyonnet, René, 'À bout de souffle', *L'Express*, 17 March 1960.

Hayward, Susan and Vincendeau, Ginette (eds), *French Film. Texts and Contexts*, London and New York: Routledge, 1990.

Hill, Leslie, '"A Form that Thinks": Godard, Blanchot, Citation', in Temple, Michael, Williams, James S. and Witt, Michael (eds), *For Ever Godard*, London: Black Dog Publishing, 2004, pp. 396–415.

Jeancolas, Jean-Pierre, *Histoire du cinéma français*, Paris: Éditions du Groupement national des cinémas de recherche, 1993.

Kreidl, John, *Jean-Luc Godard*, Boston: Twayne Publishers, 1980.

Lack, Roland François, '"Sa Voix"', in Temple, Michael, Williams, James S. and Witt, Michael (eds), *For Ever Godard*, London: Black Dog Publishing, 2004, pp. 312–329.

Lloyd, Hugh, *The Rough Guide to Gangster Movies*, London: Rough Guides, 2005.

MacCabe, Colin, *Godard: A Portrait of the Artist at 70*, London: Bloomsbury, 2003.

Macfarquhar, Larissa, 'In Quentin Tarantino's Mind the Projector Never Stops Running', *The New Yorker*, Vol. 79, issues 29–33, 20 October 2003.

Marcorelles, Louis, *Sight and Sound*, 29, Spring 1960.

Marie, Michel, '"It really makes you sick!": Jean-Luc Godard's *À bout de souffle* (1959)', in Hayward, Susan and Vincendeau, Ginette (eds), *French Film: Texts and Contexts*, London: Routledge, 1990, pp. 201–214.

Marie, Michel, '"C'est vraiment dégueulasse": Les Dialogues d'*À bout de souffle*', in Aumont, Jacques (ed.), *L'Image et la parole*, Paris: Cinémathèque française, 1999, pp. 99–111.

Marie, Michel, *À bout de souffle. Jean-Luc Godard*, Paris: Nathan, 1999.

Marie, Michel, *Comprendre Godard. Travelling avant sur* À bout de souffle *et* Le Mépris, Paris: Armand Collin, 2006.

Martin, Adrian 'Recital: Three Lyrical Interludes in Godard', in Temple, Michael, William, James S. and Witt, Michael (eds), *Forever Godard*, London: Black Dog Publishing, 2004.

Mary, Philippe, 'Cinematic Microcosm and Cultural Cosmologies – Elements of a Sociology of the New Wave', *Cinema Journal*, Vol. 49, No. 4, Summer 2010.

Maule, Rosanna, 'De-Authorizing the Auteur: Postmodern Politics of Interpellation in Contemporary European Cinema', in Degli-Esposti, Cristina (ed.), *Postmodernism in the Cinema*, New York and Oxford: Berghahn Books, 1998, pp. 113–130.

Milne, Tom (ed. and trans.), *Godard on Godard*, New York and London: Da Capo Press, 1972.

Monaco, James, *The New Wave: Truffaut, Godard, Chabrol, Rohmer, Rivette*, New York: Oxford University Press, 1976.

Moullet, Luc, 'Jean-Luc Godard', *Cahiers du cinéma*, No. 106, April 1960, pp. 25–36.

Mussman, Toby (ed.), *Jean-Luc Godard*, New York: E.P. Dutton, 1968.

Narboni, Jean and and Milne, Tom (eds), *Godard on Godard*, New York and London: Da Capo Press, 1972.

Orpen, Valerie, *Film Editing: The Art of the Expressive*, London and New York: Wallflower, 2003.

Orr, John, *Cinema and Modernity*, Cambridge: Polity Press, 1993.

Pierret, Marc 'Carnet de bord d'un apprenti cinéaste', *France-Observateur*, 29 October 1959, pp. 14–15.

Portuges, Catherine Ellen, 'Cinema and Psyche: A Psychoanalytical View of the Representation of Women in Three French Film Directors of the 1960s', PhD thesis, Los Angeles: University of California/Ann Arbor: University Microfilms International, 1982.

Predal, René, *Le Cinéma français depuis 1945*, Paris: Éditions Nathan, 1991.

Reader, Keith, 'Godard and Asynchrony' in Temple, Michael, William, James S. and Witt, Michael (eds), *Forever Godard*, London: Black Dog Publishing, 2004, pp. 72–93.

Richard, Jacques, 'La Révolution Godard', *Le Figaro*, 31 January 1985.

Richey, Jeremy, 'Glances At Undervalued Classics: Jim McBride's *Breathless* (1983)', *The Amplifier Online*, 6 August 2008.

Rochereau, Jean, *La Croix*, 30 March 1960.

Salachas, Gilbert, *Radio-Télévision-Cinéma*, 3 April 1960, p. 47.

Seguin, Louis, *Positif*, No. 33, April 1960.

Sellier, Geneviève, *Masculin Singular: French New Wave Cinema*, trans. Kristin Ross, Durham and London: Duke University Press, 2008.

Sheahan Wells, Amanda, *À bout de souffle*, York Film Notes, London: York Press/Pearson Education Ltd, 2000.

Siclier, Jacques, *Nouvelle vague?*, Paris: Les Éditions du Cerf, 1961.

Signoret, Karine 'Le beau Richard Gere: "Je ne veux pas être un sex symbol"', *France-Soir*, 6 June 1983.

Steritt, David, *The Films of Jean-Luc Godard. Seeing the Invisible*, Cambridge: Cambridge University Press, 1999.

Stevens, Brad, 'The American Friend: Tom Luddy on Jean-Luc Godard', *Senses of Cinema*, http://archive.sensesofcinema.com/contents/07/44/tom-luddy-godard.html.

Tassone, Aldo (ed.), *Que reste-t-il de la Nouvelle Vague? Chabrol, Rohmer, Truffaut, et les autres ... Inédits*, Paris: Éditions Stock, 2003.

Temple, Michael, William, James S. and Witt, Michael (eds) *Godard For Ever*, London: Black Dog Publishing, 2004.

Thompson, David, 'Once Upon a Time in Paris', *Sight and Sound*, Vol. 2, No. 5, September 1992.

Truffaut, François, 'À bout de souffle', *Radio-Cinéma-Télévision*, 4 October 1959.

Villain, Dominique, 'À bout de souffle, film "in-montable"', *Le Montage au cinéma*, Paris: Cahiers du cinéma, 1991, pp. 133–142.

Villetard, Xavier and Ventura, Claude, *Chambre 12, Hôtel de Suède: sur les traces de* À bout de souffle, film documentary 1:18':28", Arte, 1995.

Wollen, Peter, 'Godard and Counter Cinema: *Vent d'est*', *Readings and Writings: Semiotic Counter-Strategies*, London: Verso, 1982.

# Index